SCHOLASTIC

Differentiating Instruction in
Kindergarten

Cindy Middendorf

New York ■ Toronto ■ London ■ Auckland ■ Sydney
Mexico City ■ New Delhi ■ Hong Kong ■ Buenos Aires

Teaching *Resources*

Dedication

To Wayne, my husband and treasured friend.
You've given me the courage to believe in myself.
For that and so much else, I thank you.

Acknowledgments

Peggy Campbell-Rush:
You are my cheerleader, my kindred spirit,
and my inspiration. Thank you.

Janet Rhodes and Annemarie Shipman Schultheis:
You are genuine friends, respected colleagues,
and trusted voices. Thank you.

Sarah Longhi:
You are a meticulous editor, an honest guide,
and a nurturing teacher. Thank you.

My kindergarten classes at Nichols Elementary:
Each day you gave me the joy of
learning...and of teaching. Thank you.

Edited by Sarah Longhi

Cover design by Brian LaRossa
Interior design by Kelli Thompson
ISBN-13 978-0-439-87029-0
ISBN-10 0-439-87029-1

Contents

Foreword

Attempting to differentiate instruction for a classroom full of energetic, enthusiastic, developmentally different kindergartners can seem like attempting to climb Mt. Everest. Not to worry. With this book, Cindy Middendorf serves as your Sherpa, your guide, and your Sir Edmund Hillary. She has provided a map, a path, and even manageable steps for understanding differentiated instruction in kindergarten, while also holding your hand, cheering you on, and validating what you are already doing in your classroom. Indeed, Cindy acknowledges that most of what you need in order to complete the daunting task of differentiating instruction is already inside you: a caring heart and a willingness to see every child for who he or she really is.

To read *Differentiating Instruction in Kindergarten* is to spend a day in the classroom of a master teacher—Cindy welcomes readers into the world of teaching kindergarten as she would treasured friends. Her years in the classroom combined with her exceptional writing skills ensure that this is a book that will have a permanent place on your professional bookshelf. You will dog-ear pages, share this book with a friend, and buy one for a colleague, but you will never give your copy away.

Why do kindergarten teachers need this book? New and experienced teachers alike face the same dilemma as they plan meaningful instruction for our youngest primary learners: so often administrators and curriculum guides tell teachers what to do but not how to do it, and teaching with a differentiated approach is at the top of the list. Cindy helps you navigate through the terms, classifications, assessment tools, and parent communication vehicles you are expected to use—always describing how to use them in a developmentally appropriate way. You'll find many concrete, relevant techniques and examples, such as parent letters explaining the concept of differentiation, a kindergarten questionnaire that helps link children's experiences with visual representations of learning differences, and assessment tools such as the I-FAN (informal assessment notepad). These techniques not only help organize instruction effectively and respect learning differences among children; they also represent what I call the "triangle of success," the parent, teacher, and student working together for success.

After 28 years of teaching, I am rethinking and reenergizing my own instruction. I am excited to bring new ideas from this book into my own classroom to more fully educate each child to his or her full potential. I'll draw on Cindy's simple but powerful ideas—turning the occasional worksheet into a WOW sheet, using raps and rhymes for writing numbers, and learning-packed ideas for "sponge activities" that can be used throughout the school year. I love that I can refer back to Cindy's notes on her lessons and activity ideas and follow her tips to ensure that I implement them successfully and avoid possible pitfalls. I know I'll come out on the other side with each child being validated, valued, and eager to move to a new level of learning.

Climbing the Mount Everest of differentiating instruction in kindergarten? Take the first step by reading this book. Soon you will be bounding up the mountain, taking in the breathtaking views, and placing your victorious flag at the top. Thank you, Cindy, for showing us the way.

—PEGGY CAMPBELL-RUSH, M.ED.

Author of *I Teach Kindergarten, Success for Struggling Learners, Tricks of the Trade for Classroom Management, Hip-Hop Alphabop, Group Writing: How Writing Teaches Reading,* and *Reading, Writing and Word Walls*

Introduction

We are learning, although reluctantly, that the normal development of the child's brain depends upon his doing and not ours.
(From the first volume of *Practical Methods, Aids, and Devices for Teachers*, 1916)

For as long as students have shown differences in backgrounds, talents, and interests, effective teachers have instinctively tailored methods and materials to accommodate those differences. Whether in 1916 or in the twenty-first century, creative teachers have purposefully crafted instructional menus that cater to the many learning appetites in any one classroom. Differences in personalities, learning preferences, and rates of skill mastery challenge every teacher. Struggling learners need consistent success; confident learners need enrichment; all learners must be engaged.

Differentiated instruction is certainly not a new discovery or phenomenon in education, but a blend of the best practices of the one-room schoolhouse with current, research-based knowledge about learning. Carol Ann Tomlinson, author of more than one hundred books, articles, and professional development resources on differentiated instruction, acknowledges, "anything we do worthwhile in schools is inevitably a blend of old and new. The basic issues and challenges of teaching are constants. How we address those challenges evolves as our understanding of teaching and learning evolves" (*Education World*, 2006).

Volumes of research now give credibility to current and historical movements to address diverse needs. Differentiated instruction, rooted in research on learning styles, multiple intelligences, and brain-compatible strategies, is not simply the current educational buzzword. It is the essence of good teaching, espoused by respected leaders in education such as Tomlinson (1995), Eric Jensen (1998), and Geoffrey and Renate Caine (1997). The International Reading Association put forth a powerful theme to frame its annual conference in 2002: "Making a Difference Means Making It Different." Today's research continues to reaffirm what good teachers have known for years: one-size-fits-all instruction does not work at *any* grade level.

Why This Book?

In three decades of classroom teaching, twenty-two of those years in kindergarten, I lived the frustration of being given curriculum "to cover." Like experienced colleagues and novice student teachers alike, I often felt torn between "developmentally appropriate instruction" and increasingly higher academic expectations, especially in kindergarten. I quickly learned that no one recipe for instruction yields success for all, yet I was overwhelmed trying to generate all the materials and lesson plans necessary to meet all the needs of all the children.

Like many early childhood teachers, common sense and instinct guided my day-to-day teaching, and I was differentiating long before the term became synonymous with good teaching. My experience, my observations of children in my family and in my classroom, and my interest in brain-based instruction gave me the confidence to acknowledge there was no one way to teach curriculum. My class and I began to learn letters and sounds through music, art, shared reading, sign language, body formations of letters, chants, and connections to words that were important to us. Our math lessons involved building, singing, using people for manipulatives, echoing patterns, drawing, and making everyday calculations of lunch count, snacks needed, and weather graphs.

My initial readings on differentiating for process, product, and content validated my instincts. But kindergarten is a world unto itself, where the learning is *in the process*. More than any other primary grade, kindergarten teachers must instill a love of learning, a can-do attitude in each child, and a willingness to take a risk. As if that isn't enough of a challenge, we must also teach all the concepts of literacy and math that will be the solid foundation for future success. And of course, we must do it all while respecting individual differences among all the children in our classroom.

The goal of this book is to offer kindergarten teachers an understanding of differentiated instruction from the early childhood perspective and to provide a variety of strategies, activities, and management tips that will help you in differentiating your kindergarten. The book takes a seemingly overwhelming task and "chunks it down" into doable pieces for teachers in a way that demystifies differentiation for kindergarten teachers.

Teachers new to kindergarten will see the big picture and begin with a mind-set that makes differentiation a natural instructional model. Veteran teachers may recognize (and find validation in) ways in which they are already differentiating, evolve their good teaching strategies into great ones, and recharge their teaching batteries. A differentiated kindergarten is an energizing place for children and for teachers!

What This Book Offers Kindergarten Educators

Chapter 1 outlines differentiated instruction from a kindergarten perspective. You will learn the guiding principles of differentiated instruction as it applies to kindergarten and "sneak a peek" into a typical busy, buzzing kindergarten room where differences in learning styles are honored. This chapter will help you recognize that much of what you already do as a caring, insightful teacher is indeed differentiated.

Chapter 2 will refresh and refine what you learned in education classes about the many ways in which children learn. You will see examples of kindergarten children exhibiting distinct and varying modalities of learning, as well as children demonstrating each of the multiple intelligences. You will even be asked to take a look at your own modalities of learning. This chapter will also help you understand why it is difficult to pinpoint modalities and intelligences at the kindergarten level, and will ease fears about the need to do so.

In Chapter 3, you'll discover ways to build a profile for each child without "pigeonholing" each. You'll find tips for using parent input to better know each child and checklists to help you understand the unique and emerging learning style of each child. Also in Chapter 3, you'll find strategies for using formal and informal assessment tools, along with literacy and math checklists for kindergarten.

Chapter 4 describes simple, step-by-step ways to begin differentiating in your kindergarten classroom. You'll learn how to get parents and children on board with the idea that not all children will be doing the same thing at the same time. You'll explore ways to manage your classroom that will allow you to concentrate on teaching so that all may learn. This chapter also includes specific differentiated activities that will keep children engaged and learning while you are working one-on-one or in small groups.

Chapter 5 is packed with ideas to motivate children, teach key skills, and meet diverse needs. The chapter offers suggestions for addressing and accommodating the wide range of skills and maturities in your classroom, including fine-motor, vision, early literacy, and math readiness. You'll find innovative and inexpensive ways to design and differentiate centers as well as whole-group instruction.

Throughout the book, real samples of real kindergartners at work illustrate differentiation in action: in classroom scenarios, in photographs, and in student work. Also sprinkled throughout the book are references and resources that provide a research-based rationale for differentiated instruction and give you options for further learning. Teachers, like children, approach learning in diverse ways. Whether you have taught for decades or for days, or are anticipating your first teaching assignment, I hope this book gives you the confidence to always put the children, one by one, ahead of the curriculum.

Chapter 1

What Does Differentiated Instruction Mean in Kindergarten?

You teach kindergarten. Lucky you! There are few other places in the universe where there is such honesty, love of learning, self-acceptance, intrinsic motivation, and sheer joy in living. As a caring kindergarten teacher, you receive a healthy daily dose of ego building from children who adore you. If only they knew how you agonize over creating a nurturing world where each of them can learn, blossom, and flourish at their own rate.

Kindergarten teachers have always wanted each child to feel valued, confident, and successful. When we let our common sense direct our teaching, children bloom. Yet in today's standards-driven, assessment-dependent, "push-down" curriculum world, conscientious teachers often feel like jugglers keeping too many balls in the air: addressing standards, accommodating IEP's, balancing parent expectations, keeping abreast of new research, and managing a classroom of unpredictable live wires. Common sense tells us that the most important ball to hold in the air is the child. We frequently become frustrated when the other demands on our time and energy keep us from doing what we do best: nurture the love of learning in children.

Differentiated instruction is a philosophy, a way of thinking and structuring our classrooms that puts children first. It lets a child's success be measured by his or her own individual growth. It allows a teacher to step back, survey an active, buzzing classroom and say,

"Yes!" Because early childhood teachers are so in tune with children's developmental stages, chances are that you already employ a lot of the rock-solid principles of differentiated instruction:

- Do you have high expectations for all children?

- Do you model respect for all children's work?

- Do you consciously integrate physical movement, music, and art into lessons?

- Do you have free-play centers for building, drawing, reading, imagining, and exploring?

- Do your children have choices in materials, centers, and assignments?

- Do you use time flexibly?

- Do you incorporate whole-group instruction, small-group instruction, and one-on-one instruction?

- Is the composition of your small groups flexible and ever changing?

- Do you use ongoing, authentic assessment and "kid-watching" to adjust and evaluate teaching as well as learning?

- Do you assess children according to their individual growth?

- Are your children relaxed, eager, and actively engaged?

- Are there times in your room when children are working on several different activities?

- Do you vary your teaching style, ask open-ended questions, and initiate discussions?

- Are children involved in classroom problem solving?

Chances are that you answered yes to most of these. Kindergarten teachers instinctively know that each child is unique. Congratulations! You will not need to reinvent the wheel to differentiate your classroom. You will validate the effective teaching strategies you already employ, focus on making your good teaching better, and celebrate the strengths and successes of all your students.

The Instructional Menu: Serving All Appetites

Current research is making us increasingly aware of the importance of recognizing and honoring the uniqueness of each learner. Every kindergarten teacher acknowledges, struggles with, and works endlessly to accommodate widely differing strengths, needs, personalities, and developmental levels in one classroom. Most teachers of young children can competently discuss auditory, visual, and kinesthetic modalities of learning. Likewise, we all have been schooled in Gardner's theory of multiple intelligences (1993 and 2000). Yet understanding these differences in our children is easier than supporting these differences. Differentiated instruction reinforces children's strengths, allows different children to be mastering skills in different ways, and encourages children to explore and process information through varying learning preferences (modalities). Chapter 2 will help you to recognize the preferred modalities of learning among your students and to identify the intelligences within your classroom. The caveat is acknowledging that the younger the children, the less defined those modalities and intelligences are.

Differentiated instruction is more than just having different students involved in different activities. Differentiated instruction means that the teacher has consciously tried to engage children in learning and reinforcing skills through an array of methods while addressing curriculum standards. Differentiated instruction means that one instructional goal or objective can be attained using different strategies, different contents, and/or different finished products for different children. Eric Jensen, an expert in the exploding field of brain research, notes that "the more ways we learn something, in more situations, with more intelligences, more emotions, more forms of media," the more likely we will embed that learning (1997).

Sound overwhelming?

With so many children processing information in so many different ways (modalities), with so many different strengths (intelligences), at so many different rates (skill levels), and at so many different levels of maturity (developmental ages), what's a teacher to do? In addition to the normal range of learning preferences, and the normal bell curve of abilities, an increasing number of special-needs students are being integrated into traditional classrooms.

Most teachers have little background for dealing with special needs, few on-site resources for support, and too little time in the school day to meet the demands. Sadly, the task overwhelms many teachers who then fall back to the traditional comfort zone: one-size-fits-all teacher-designed activities that all children must complete.

Totally differentiating every lesson every day for every student is unrealistic. Yet as we learn more and more about the brain development of youngsters and understand how neural pathways are constructed, we cannot ignore the unique strengths and needs of each child.

Validate Yourself: You're Already Differentiating!

Now for the good news: once familiar with differentiated instruction, most kindergarten teachers will realize they are already instinctively differentiating in small ways. Early childhood educators are masters at intuitively sensing children's unique strengths and needs. Teachers who use a variety of instructional methods (whole group, small group, one-on-one, and independent learning centers) already know that some children learn best in one arena and others in another. Learning centers, long an integral piece of most kindergarten classrooms, provided differentiated instruction long before differentiated instruction was a research-based best practice.

More good news: once a teacher begins to use some basic strategies for differentiation, the enthusiasm and success of the students bring the joy back to teaching. And differentiating your kindergarten instruction is not difficult! The more ways a kindergartner is exposed to a skill, concept, or idea, using different intelligences, in different situations, with different materials, the more the learning is internalized. When Anna paints a sunflower,

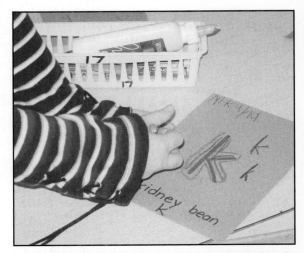

A child-friendly approach to handwriting practice: As a class, the children repeatedly trace the prewritten *k*, first with a finger and then with crayons as they repeat the letter name and sound., "This is /k/-/k/-/k/, *k*." They trace around the *k* and practice making the *k* without tracing. Finally, in the Letter Center, they trace with glue, and affix kidney beans to reinforce the letter sound.

hears a story about a sunflower, sequences the growth of a sunflower, writes a sentence about a sunflower, sings and uses her body to show sunflower growth, picks the seeds from a sunflower head and uses them in an art project, Anna knows sunflowers! When Kenny practices sight words by playing bingo with sight words, writing sight words with magnetic letters, using chants and cheers to spell sight words, and highlighting sight words in print, Kenny learns sight words. Children of all learning strengths and skill levels find success when a caring teacher designs a learning smorgasbord.

A Look Inside a Differentiated Kindergarten

It is 10:20 A.M. A busy hum is heard as children move about and interact with materials, other children, and their teacher, Ms. K. The lesson begins on the story rug as Ms. K reads aloud from the nonfiction big book, *A Butterfly Is Born* by Melvin Berger. After the reading, the children curl up on the rug like tiny caterpillar eggs. At Ms. K's direction, they "hatch" and immediately "eat" their tiny eggshells. They continue to play-act, munching their way around a leaf and spinning themselves into chrysalises. Once they emerge as graceful butterflies, they glide on silent wings around the room and come to light on the rug where they sing the "Butterfly Song."

Now all are engaged in varying related activities in the room. Some are working with butterfly sequencing puzzles; others are at the easels painting the life stages of the butterfly. A group is in the Book Nook, poring over butterfly, moth, and insect books, and using tracing paper to reproduce pictures. A few are at the clay table designing caterpillars and butterflies. Ms. K is circulating, staying especially close to those who are at the writing center putting finishing touches on their butterfly sentences.

In a few minutes, Ms. K will once again gather the children on the rug where today's Shared Reading lesson will focus on finding sight words and rhyming words in a poem about butterflies.

At the kindergarten level, children are still exploring and establishing their own preferred modalities and intelligences. Although young children from an early age give unmistakable signs of preferred intelligences and modalities, most eagerly explore all arenas of their world through all their senses. Like sponges, they absorb information easily and are willing to move outside of their own comfort zone (take a risk) to learn. In our kindergarten instruction, we should be presenting the same information in a variety of ways, engaging all the modalities as we present information. For skill practice and reinforcement, we need to offer such a variety that children have opportunities to explore all modalities and to reinforce their strongest modality whenever possible. However, most children will joyfully embrace all activities you present, as long as those activities are developmentally appropriate. Young children will eagerly devour all that is offered on the instructional buffet table, and eventually, most will settle into those types of activities that best satisfy their own appetites.

Whenever you teach a concept in a variety of ways, you greatly increase the chances of reaching each student. You multiply the chances that each student will remember what you have taught, since you have created many neurological pathways to access the same information. Then, when you match the reinforcing and enrichment activities to the child's learning preferences, learning happens effortlessly.

Differentiated instruction incorporates a smorgasbord of teaching methods, a variety of tools and materials, and a spectrum of curricular themes matched to the needs and levels of the learners. It means finding the switch that "turns on" each student. It means moving away from the traditional one-size-fits-all design and timing of instruction.

Differentiated instruction in kindergarten (or any grade level) is not ability grouping, nor is it a commercially prepared, scripted program. Although a differentiated classroom is actively buzzing, it is not chaotic or unmanaged. Groups are flexible and ever changing, rather than homogeneously rigid. While we effectively offer varying levels of material, differentiation is much more than a diet of enrichment for more-ready learners and constant repetition for learners needing more support.

> ### ■ Brain Fact
>
> When learning occurs, cells are stimulated to grow branch-like extensions called dendrites. Each dendrite provides another pathway with which connections can be made. What we call "greater depth of meaning" simply means cells making more connections and new pathways to other cells. The secret is to provide multiple contexts for learning the same thing. Jensen, *Brain Compatible Strategies*, 1997

The joy of learning, the growth of self-confidence, and the willingness to take a risk are the ultimate measures of success in kindergarten.

Wise is the teacher who views a classroom through the eyes of a five-year-old, and wise is the teacher who realizes that not all five-year-old eyes view the world in the same way. Lucky are the five-year-olds whose teacher sees each one as able!

As we begin to differentiate our classrooms, we give our children and ourselves permission to focus on long-term goals. Instead of "How do I fit it all in today?" we begin to ask, "Where in the curriculum does everyone need to be at the end of this week (month, quarter, semester)?" Then we can plan several routes to reach that goal. Like travelers, some children will arrive at the destination via the scenic route, some by highway, and some by air, train, or bicycle. The journey for each should reinforce the joy of travel, and ultimately, the joy of reaching the destination.

Chapter 2

Modalities & Intelligences: The Channels for Learning

Every child deserves a chance to succeed. Teachers must make a genuine effort not only to assess current skill levels, but also to provide instruction in multiple modalities, engaging a variety of intelligences. What is the difference between a modality and an intelligence? How crucial is it to identify each child's learning preferences and intelligences in kindergarten? How can we be confident that we are giving each child the best possible scenario for learning? It's simpler than you think. Let's revisit all those college classes on learning, but this time through our kindergarten eyes.

How Are Modalities of Learning Different From Intelligences?

A modality of learning is a way in which we process and understand information that is presented to us, a route through which we subconsciously choose to interpret stimuli and make sense of the world around us. Our preferred modality of learning helps us to concentrate and move from concrete to abstract thinking. *Although we tend to have one modality that is most comfortable, all humans take in information through all modalities,* a fact especially important for teachers to remember.

An intelligence is an innate talent or strength. We use our intelligences to demonstrate our understanding of the world as well as to organize the information that our senses feed to us. Our choices, our hobbies, and our careers often reflect our intelligences. Most adults—and children—have strengths in more than one area of intelligence. As teachers we must understand that a child may have intelligences that have not been developed simply because he has not had the opportunities to explore his world in multiple ways.

When we stay mindful of modalities and intelligences, we become more aware of how and what we are offering our kindergarten children instructionally. Once we are comfortable with these powerful indicators, we can tailor our classrooms to fit the needs of all children.

Modalities of Learning

The concept of modalities of learning is a complex, multi-faceted one with reams of research (Grinder, *Righting the Educational Conveyor Belt*, 1989). For our kindergarten purposes (as well as our sanity) we will focus on the four primary means of gathering and processing information. We can effectively differentiate by acknowledging that children—and adults—are typically visual learners, auditory learners, kinesthetic learners, or tactile learners. Many experts in the area agree that there is much overlap between the kinesthetic and the tactile modalities, and some theorists lump the two together. The fine distinction is that strictly tactile learners need active hands-on learning. Truly kinesthetic learners think best when their entire body is in motion.

The secret of education lies in respecting the student.
—RALPH WALDO EMERSON

Researchers in the arena of modalities of learning have further identified conscious, subconscious, and unconscious preferences (Markova, *How Your Child Is Smart*, 1992), as well as sensory and intuitive learning styles (Silver, 2003). Such multilevel, detailed analysis, while interesting and enlightening, is overkill in kindergarten (or sure to kill the kindergarten teacher!).

Lydia: A Visual Learner

Lydia processes information well in the visual mode. She more easily remembers what she has seen than what she has heard. Lydia likes to sit in the front during a read-aloud, so that she can clearly see the pictures. She'll often say, "Come see what I did," rather than describe what she did. Lydia can quickly zero in on details in print and pictures. She enjoys "find the hidden objects" activities. She is easily distracted by a lot of clutter or movement around her. Lydia best remembers what she can see and visually study.

Jake: An Auditory Learner

Jake prefers learning in the auditory mode. He often mumbles to himself while playing or working and enjoys songs, chants, and rhythmic language activities. He is good at imitating sounds and others' tone of voice. Phonemic awareness comes easily to him. Jake will sometimes say, "I can't think. It's too noisy." He likes being read to, listening to story telling, and hearing books on tape. Jake will quickly ask a friend or teacher to explain something when he is unsure. Jake remembers best that which he hears.

Taylor: A Tactile Learner

Taylor, a tactile learner, touches everything in her environment, including people. She likes to play with the long hair of the friend sitting in front of her on the rug. She quickly learns weaving, shoe tying, and other fine-motor skills. She doodles, twists a button, or plays with her shoelaces when listening to a story. Taylor loves to play with interlocking cubes, dress paper dolls, and use magnetic drawing toys. She appears to listen during whole group activities, but she seldom remembers what was said. Taylor remembers best that which she has touched or handled.

Miguel: A Kinesthetic Learner

Miguel is predominantly a kinesthetic learner. For Miguel, even sitting still involves a lot of moving, although he is not hyperactive. He uses a lot of hand gestures as he speaks, touches other children often, and wants to dive right into a project before directions are given. Miguel has strong large-muscle coordination, but messy, oversized handwriting. Like our tactile learner Taylor, Miguel likes concrete, touchable learning activities. He sometimes calls to you, "Watch me!" especially on the playground or during a gross-motor activity. You notice that Miguel often stands as he cuts, traces, or works at a center. For Miguel, learning is best remembered when he moves as he is learning.

Which child is the most intelligent? Which is most ready for reading instruction? Which is most likely to find success on the literacy journey? Clearly, a preferred learning modality is no indication of intelligence, readiness, or potential. However, research tells us that honoring those learning preferences will allow each child to use his or her natural talents to enrich learning.

Yet is it reasonable to ask a kindergarten teacher to determine and pronounce a preferred modality for each young learner? Certainly our instruction must begin long before we have had a chance to observe each child in the context of the school community. Can we effectively provide an enriching environment even before we know that Jeremy is a visual learner or that Marianna prefers the auditory mode? What if we make a mistake and continually encourage a child to learn through a modality that is not his strongest? Is it possible that a child could be comfortable in all modalities?

Relax, take a breath, and know that providing opportunities for *all* learners to learn through *all* modalities can only enrich each child's experience. Our job is to be aware of and tuned in to the fact that children process information in different ways. Our goal is to provide instruction that engages children through many hooks so that all children have the best possible chance of embedding learning. In doing so, we also encourage children to explore outside of their own comfort zone.

We teachers are wise to analyze our own learning styles. We comfortably present materials in a way that makes sense to us. In doing so, we may unintentionally shortchange more than half of our class. None of us would insist that a child become a vegetarian simply because Teacher is, or play tennis each day simply because Teacher loves tennis. Complete the following survey to help you determine your preferred modality of learning. Then carefully consider your instructional approach in whole-group, small-group, and center activities. Do most of your activities teach to the children who learn in your preferred modality? It's time to see the world through the eyes of the rest of the children!

Learning Style Survey for Teachers

1. When I spell, I
    a. see the word in my head
    b. sound the word out phonetically
    c. write it with a finger on my palm to see if it feels right
    d. imagine feeling the letters on the keyboard as I type it

2. I learn well through
    a. a PowerPoint and/or handout presentation
    b. a lecture approach when the speaker uses varying voice, inflection, and so on
    c. an out-of-seat, moving activity
    d. an activity that keeps my hands busy: taking notes, doodling, manipulating materials

3. I can follow directions best if I
    a. see them written down
    b. hear them given step by step
    c. can be involved in a demonstration of them
    d. write them down myself

4. I most enjoy playing/doing
    a. solitaire, concentration, memory match
    b. name that tune, mad-libs, word games
    c. charades, dodge ball, yoga
    d. checkers; jigsaw puzzles; drawing, painting, or sculpting

5. When I shop, I
    a. am attracted by colors, attractive displays, bold signage
    b. have an ongoing conversation in my head about everything I
        see, or I think aloud to my companion
    c. walk around a large area before I zero in on a specific section
    d. touch lots of items, even those I have no intention of buying

6. When I have business to conduct, I prefer to
    a. arrange a face-to-face meeting
    b. call on the telephone
    c. move, walk, and talk while with my contact person
    d. doodle, play with a paper clip, or twist a pen while talking

Mostly (a) answers indicate a visual learner, (b) answers point to a strong auditory modality, (c) answers support kinesthetic learning, and (d) answers show a preference for tactile experiences. Not surprisingly, most adults find overlapping modalities—proof positive that we are well-rounded, integrated learners!

How do we know we are providing a balance of modality-friendly kindergarten activities? Examine the following, and design a classroom setting in which you are using strategies from each modality daily.

In a perfect world, the preferred modalities for all our children would be as easy to identify as eye color. In the real kindergarten world, those preferred modalities are vaguely displayed. Yes, we need to keep eyes wide open for emerging patterns. No, we need not expend inordinate effort with elaborate assessment tools. Instead of asking, "What is this child's strongest modality of learning?" we need to ask, "Am I incorporating a wide range of activities that satisfy all learning modalities? Will all children engage in a wonder-filled array of learning activities and instructional approaches?"

Once we are tuned into the wide range of learning modalities, we also need to examine the broad spectrum of natural intelligences with which our children demonstrate understanding. Once again, the more we understand the multiple intelligences, the more likely we are to offer experiences and assessments that allow all children to succeed.

Multiple Intelligences

Much has been wrangled, researched, and written about multiple intelligences since Gardner made the term a well-accepted educational theory in his *Frames of Mind* (1983). Prior to Gardner's work, most educators accepted that intelligence centered primarily around verbal and math ability, resulting in a fixed IQ score that does nothing to represent strengths in other important areas. Current brain research supports the concept of multiple intelligences, and few teachers would argue. To better serve your students, to better understand their behaviors, and to tailor your menu of instruction, you need to observe the strengths of each.

If children grew up according to early indications, we should have nothing but geniuses.

–JOHANN WOLFGANG VON GOETHE

Often a child's strengths are obvious at an early age. Parents notice that their toddler learns new words and speaks with inflection before her peers or are amazed that their ten-month-old will deftly climb out of the crib. However, most children's unique mix of strengths and learning preferences becomes more obvious after they enter school, where they freely explore realms that may have been unavailable to them in their early environment. Parents who have a passion for music and theater may have provided a wealth of those very enriching experiences for their preschooler. That lucky youngster may come to school with a passion for the performing arts, yet once exposed to team sports, may also find an aptitude for athletics.

When it comes to differentiated instruction, the kindergarten teacher needs to take a broad view, assuming a potential strength in every intelligence for every student. So while it is important to be knowledgeable about the multiple intelligences and to be alert for the signs in our children, we need to use caution. Kindergarten is a time for a child to explore all his intelligences, to learn that he has strengths in several areas, and to be excited about learning. Our goal is a paradox: to satisfy the hunger, but also to whet the appetite. Not all children will demonstrate an intelligence as obviously as those introduced in the following snippets.

Verbal-Linguistic Intelligence

Jamal is five, but he has been speaking articulately for two years. His family calls him "gabby." He loves to tell, retell, and make up stories. He enjoys learning new words and easily remembers vocabulary. When he asks, "Why?" he expects and will comprehend a complex answer. Word games are fun for Jamal: rhyming, riddles, and fill-in-the-blanks trigger his enthusiasm.

Bodily-Kinesthetic Intelligence

Donette does not appear physically strong, but she is very well coordinated and limber, both in fine-muscle and gross-muscle use. She can stand on one foot with excellent balance. With minimum coaching, she quickly learned to ride a two-wheeler, to jump rope, and to cross the monkey bars. Donette is well coordinated and walked up stairs using alternate feet at an early age.

Logical-Mathematic Intelligence

Sharese is good at sorting and classifying. She can tell you that seemingly different objects have certain traits in common. Once patterns have been introduced in class, she seems to find them everywhere. She likes orderliness, and is good at strategy games like checkers. Sharese can easily see the information provided in a graph and draw conclusions from the data. She understands cause and effect and prefers logical explanations for her questions. Sharese likes every question to have a correct answer.

Using screwdrivers and pliers at the Take Apart Center to dismantle a discarded remote-control car encourages interpersonal, logical, and bodily-kinesthetic intelligences. The bonus: it's fun! (Note the safety glasses.)

Intrapersonal Intelligence

Daniel often happily chooses to play alone and is self-directed. He watches others and will join in when asked, but he is perfectly comfortable working independently. He can tell you how he feels about things, and he can accurately tell you what he personally is good at and what he needs help with. He is adamant about his likes and dislikes. His strong will has led his family to label him "stubborn." Often, when asked, "What are you doing?" Daniel will reply, "Just thinking."

Interpersonal Intelligence

Lexi established herself early as a kindergarten class leader. Most of the other children want to be near her in morning circle, sit by her at lunch, and be her partner for activities. Lexi is usually kind to other children and respectful of their feelings. She makes friends easily and interacts confidently with peers and adults. She loves her friends, is nurturing and is often the peacemaker on the playground. Lexi has a strong sense of justice and wants the world to be fair.

Constructing with building manipulatives individually or in a group, fosters visual-spatial intelligence and allows children to imagine, plan, and create. As they discuss their designs, they practice communicating ideas and employing visual imagery.

Visual-Spatial Intelligence

Wayne is creative with building blocks, clay, and 3-D models. He draws often, and his sketches have a lot of detail. He wants to see a sample of any finished product before he starts his own. He also works successfully on computer activities. During free-choice time, he chooses puzzles, mazes, and "put together" type toys. His parents complain that he takes everything apart!

Musical Intelligence

Adam hums while he works. When the class is singing, he eagerly participates and is almost always on key. He regularly plays a pretend guitar, drum, or piano and really enjoys rhythmic clapping as well as echo songs and games. Adam loves to dance, and he has surprising coordination and tempo. Adam remembers songs and melodies that he learned in preschool.

Naturalist Intelligence

Gretchen has earned the nickname, "The Bug Girl." She is usually in the grass on the playground watching critters. Gretchen is keenly aware of her surroundings and is the first to notice if you have changed the picture on your desk. She easily adapts to change, displays common sense, and has a lot of interest in the patterns of nature.

Not surprisingly, the children who demonstrate verbal-linguistic and logical-mathematical intelligence have an advantage in the traditional classroom. Our educational system is skewed to these

Strategies to Engage All Learners

To engage visual learners

Use highlighting tape in text
Make reference to posters and visuals around the room
Point on the map when referencing different states, countries
Show filmstrips, videotapes
Diagram a story through a story web
Use expressive body language and gestures
Point out details in photos and illustrations
Display word walls for themes, sight words, names

To engage auditory learners

Read aloud often
Offer a listening center
Teach rhymes for making numbers, letters
Sing to learn skills
Vary pitch and tone of voice
Encourage retellings and Readers Theater
Provide puppets
Demonstrate use of phonics phones

To engage kinesthetic and tactile learners

Model role-playing and acting out
Use gross-motor activities to reinforce concepts
Allow active participation in experiments and demonstrations
Provide props for story retelling
Encourage standing when answering questions
Practice writing in cornmeal, sand, or salt
Make music, rhythm, and keeping the beat an integral part of lessons
Supply clay, acetate sheets, and whiteboards for writing practice

children. Yet we have all heard the story of Einstein, who was deemed "slow," and whose parents worried because his language development was so delayed. History offers up other brilliant people who seemingly struggled through school but showed remarkable talent once their own intelligences were nurtured. Quite likely, their genius was apparent at an early age but was not honored by the schooling required of them. Can you imagine being the early childhood teacher of Einstein who told his parents that poor Albert probably would not ever learn like other children because he was "backward"?

The modalities and intelligences of children are the avenues down which our instruction must travel to arrive at the ultimate destination: solid mastery of skills, concepts, and understandings. And, just as "all roads lead to Rome," multiple pathways lead to that goal, and different children will travel better on different routes.

We know that modalities of learning matter and that all children need to be exposed to all modalities. We know that individual intelligences matter and that all children need to explore many intelligences. So, is it important to build an individual learning profile for each student? How would we go about doing it? Is the profile worth the time and effort expended? In Chapter 3, we'll take a practical, realistic look at building learning profiles for children.

Chapter 3

Building a Profile for Your Learners

Differentiating in the classroom is an ever-evolving, spiraling learning curve for teachers as well as for children. The better we know our learners, the better we can facilitate their success. Instead of administering only quarterly assessments in order to fill out a report card, teachers in differentiated kindergartens gather information about each child in an ongoing, systematic fashion. The goal is to see "the big picture," the child as a sum total of his or her social, emotional, physical, and learning being, not simply as a collector of skills.

In this chapter, we will look at building a learning profile for each student: what to include, how to assemble the pieces, and how to use the information. We will examine quick, efficient strategies for recording informal observations, gathering parent input, and using formal assessments. We will also consider the role of portfolios as a piece of the profile, as well as student self-assessment.

Education is not the filling of a bucket, but the lighting of a fire.
—WILLIAM BUTLER YEATS

What is a Learning Profile?

A learning profile is a collection of information that helps a teacher evaluate and understand a child's progress and plan instruction that is most effective. A profile gives evidence of skills, strengths, needs, and interests, as well as how those evolve over time in your classroom. A profile of a child as a learner includes:

- Informal teacher observations about skills, modalities, and intelligences, noted as the child is working and playing;

- Parent input;

- Feedback from other adults who interact regularly with the child (gym teacher, aide, librarian, nurse);

■ Formal assessment results; and

■ Dated samples of student work, including self-assessment pieces.

Later in the chapter, we will take a closer look at each of these components, how to effectively gather them, and how each is important in building a comprehensive view of the child.

A profile is not necessarily *one* folder or *one* file. Pieces of a child's profile may be stored physically in different areas. For instance, standardized test scores, copies of reports from preschool, and health and medical records may be in an official permanent folder that must be kept locked in a file cabinet; informal notes and teacher observations may be in folders marked with students' first names and stored in a file box; student work samples may be stored in expanding folders or pizza boxes. When all pieces are considered, the teacher has a complete profile, or picture of the child as a learner.

Because so much of the profile depends on observations, and because children grow, change, and learn daily, a learner's profile is never really "finished." Specific pieces such as kindergarten screening results may be available to you before you meet the child. (More about kindergarten screenings later in this chapter.) But the substance of the profile will be what you gather as the year progresses. For some children (those with exceptional skills or behaviors, suspected learning disabilities, or notable family news that impacts the child) you may add notes on a daily or weekly basis, save lots of student work, or conference with parents often. Those profiles will accumulate pieces quickly. However, all profiles will grow throughout the year. Just as a child's pediatrician gathers and compares health data over time and may change prescriptions or courses of treatment, a child's teacher must look at the cumulative data and be willing to adjust his or her thinking about children as the year marches on.

Why is it important to create a learning profile for each student?

Assessment is crucial for differentiation. Why assess? It seems obvious that we need to know what children know. In the old days of "here's the curriculum; now teach it," children's achievement was largely judged according to the achievement of other children at that grade level. The most relevant indicator of a child's success was his or her rank in the classroom or according to state or national norms. In today's standards-driven educational environment, those numbers are still an important part of the learning profile. However, with current research supporting more child-centered, *differentiated* education, teachers are realizing that achievement must be monitored in a variety of ways that gauge each child's individual growth, and they plan instruction that will best support the child as he or she takes the next step in learning.

The Whys of Assessment

ASSESSMENT DATA HELPS US:	TEACHER REFLECTIONS
1. For each child, define instructional areas that need adjustment, reinforcement, extension, or challenge.	*Janet already knows sets and numbers to 10. I can encourage her to begin writing the number words for the sets when we're practicing.*
2. Plan group activities and individual mini-lessons that target specific areas for growth.	*Both Hunter and Liam are still naming /g/ with the /j/ sound. I'll pull them aside during center time and do a follow-up lesson.*
3. Celebrate and nurture the child's own development, and include the child in that awareness.	*Kenny! Look at the way you are writing your name now. Just last week, you weren't happy with how it looked. You have worked hard, and it shows!*
4. Effectively communicate to parents about progress and achievement.	*Look at these two math work samples, dated six weeks apart. Sherelle has gone from simply identifying a pattern to now extending and creating her own patterns!*
5. Evaluate and revise our plans for instruction based on student needs.	*Seventeen children are still mixing up the nickel and the quarter. I need to reteach that in another way and give them more practice.*

Learning about a child through his or her profile will help you motivate the child because you will better understand his or her interests and hobbies. It will help you plan instruction for the child and the group as a whole when you are aware of common backgrounds, needs, and strengths among children. A profile will compel you to consider the big picture instead of isolated skills as you plan your teaching.

In addition, the profile will help you track how children have grown, direct parent conferences and reports, and offer recommendations for next year's teacher.

Informal Assessments: Lots of Places to Look

Kindergarten teachers must assess readiness, learning preferences, and skill levels in language, concepts, and motor areas to effectively build a program that moves all children along on the learning train. Having a sense of a child's preferred modality of learning and natural intelligence(s) is helpful, but conclusively identifying those for each child is unrealistic and certainly unnecessary in creating a differentiated kindergarten classroom. We need to hit the ground running early in the year, long before we have learned about each child's learning preferences.

Ongoing Assessment: Real, Reliable, and Revealing

Ongoing assessment is in-the-moment assessment that focuses on a child in a natural classroom situation. While formal skill assessments are a valuable piece of the overall learning profile, a global, ongoing, anecdotal picture is a more accurate indicator of progress and is more likely to drive child-centered instruction. Ongoing assessments are more authentic and less stressful for the child, since the child often is unaware that he or she is being assessed. Unlike many formal assessments, ongoing assessment does not involve tests, percentiles, or scripted directions. Instead, a teacher consciously looks for and makes notes about a child's specific behavior, choice, oral language, reaction, or demonstration of skill *as it is noticed* (or as soon as possible after), whether it is on the playground, in the classroom, or in the hallway. In a differentiated classroom, the teacher becomes very good at noting moments that give a glimpse into a child's learning process. The younger the child, the more appropriate it is to use this kind of observational assessment (Katz, 1997).

Ongoing assessment results in short, cryptic notes that you jot on a sticky pad or handy sheet while that observation is fresh in your mind (or as soon as possible). The wording and reference may be something that only you will understand, but it will be enough to trigger the thought afterward when you review it, whether it is that day after school, several days later, or next week as you prepare for a parent conference. (More later on how to keep track of all those notable moments.) Following are examples of "internal teacher talk" you might be thinking as you make notes of things you want to remember:

"9/23 Kylie: block tower—a-b-a-b pattern." You notice that during free-play time, Kylie used colored inch cubes to create a simple pattern. Kylie had also turned to her playmate and pointed out the pattern and even called it an a-b-a-b- pattern. She then continued to extend the pattern. You now know that Kylie has mastered a-b patterning!

"9/13 Jeremy: cutting with left; coloring right. Dominance?" You see that Jeremy used his left hand for cutting but his right for coloring. This may be a fluke, but you consciously note it, since you want to remember to watch to see if it is a consistent behavior that needs addressing.

"9/23 Karen: black/brown?" Karen holds up her black crayon when you ask all children to hold up the brown. You think it was Karen who did that yesterday, but you didn't have a chance to note it. Today, you and her classmates help her correct the mistake at that moment, but you want to remember to check again later. Does Karen really need reteaching of those two colors?

Of course, a teacher could be overwhelmed trying to note every interesting behavior, reaction, or skill performance for every child every day. Too much emphasis on "kid-watching" could have us not seeing the forest for the trees. However, ongoing assessment is integral, especially early in the year when we are getting to know children. We need to make a conscious effort to learn something new about each child within the first two weeks of school. It should be done more often than formal assessment and have equal (or greater) impact on decisions that are made concerning a child's placement and instruction. Ongoing, observational assessment should also be used as an important part of what we report to parents.

How do I do manage all that kid-watching?

For a perceptive teacher, always on the lookout for evidence of growth, alert surveillance becomes the most reliable tool for building a profile for every child. Countless times during the day, we notice behaviors, overhear noteworthy kid comments, or make mental notes about children. Unfortunately, most of us have little time to record, flesh out, or ponder those instant observations, and those gems are quickly forgotten. In a differentiated classroom, the teacher understands how powerful those incidental observations may be and makes a deliberate effort to notice and keep track of what he or she sees.

An easy, informal, at-your-fingertips method of recording what you see when you see it will serve you well in identifying skill needs, as well as learning preferences and intelligences. Whatever method you choose, it must be simple for *you* to use. The easier it is for you to record what you notice as you notice it, the more authentic and reliable your assessment will be.

A teacher eager to know all he or she can know about each student becomes attached to an "I-FAN" (informal assessment notepad). Your I-FAN must be designed by you to fit your teaching style, your organizational preferences, and your chosen technique for recording information.

Think of your I-FAN as your personal, private classroom journal. Don't worry about phrasing, using professional jargon, or analyzing. Jot down the date along with a word or key phrase that will trigger the specifics when you come back to it later. The more you use it, the better you will become at zeroing in on what is important, and creating your own shorthand language for yourself (such as writing "ctr" for "center"). When you later transfer information into the child's folder, onto a parent conference form, or as anecdotal record, you can polish it. Be direct and obvious in your comments. Your I-FAN is for your eyes only!

Several techniques and formats for an I-FAN will help you record and organize observations:

- Some teachers carry index cards on an O-ring, each labeled with the name of a student, providing ready access to the I-FAN. The stack of cards is usually in the teacher's pocket, or she may have several: one at the rug area, one at small group area, and one on her desk. Whenever she notices a significant behavior or has a brainstorm of an idea to try with a specific child, she makes a quick note. ("10/22 Frustrated with pencil . . . Need foam grip?") Use four or five different colors alternately in the stack of cards, and you'll soon be adept at finding cards quickly. ("I know Timmy's is green . . . near the back of the stack.") Leave a few blank white cards with no child's name attached for you to make general notes to yourself when you have a passing thought that merits further pondering. ("9/4 Colors on filters— eye droppers?" to remind yourself that your lesson on combining colors might work better with eye droppers, food coloring, and coffee filters.)

■ Some teachers prefer a never-far-from-reach clipboard or notebook as an I-FAN. It could be a folder that has a pencil attached with a string and a stack of sticky notes. A quick note on the pad, a second to slap the note onto the clipboard or folder, and instant assessment notes!

■ Some teachers carry a small reporter's tape recorder in their pocket to record observations and actually "talk to themselves" for later review.

I-FAN: An O-ring with colored index cards is a portable, simple tool for recording on-the-spot observations.

The device you choose for your informal assessment notes is not as important as using it. Take the clipboard (or cards, or recorder) to the playground and other unstructured areas where you can unobtrusively watch children.

How many notes should I take on each child? How often?

Your purpose is to notice patterns of behaviors ("This is the fourth note I have in here about Ian refusing to stop a center and clean up"), remind yourself of questions you'd like answered about a child ("Are they really moving to Italy as he says they are?"), and record specifics to reinforce what you report to parents ("I need his family's help. I've noted six specific examples of Ike's acting aggressively when he is frustrated.")

We do not have the time (or the energy!) to actively seek out things to write about each child every day. Neither can we stop to analyze, ponder, or investigate each time we notice something that catches our attention. However, when we observe a peculiar behavior, hear a revealing remark, or see an unusual interaction between children, we can make a quick note, enough to remind us later that day or that week of something we wanted to reflect upon. For some children, you will collect lots of little notes quickly!

On the other hand, no notes written for several weeks about a child may mean that the child has done or said nothing remarkable, or it may mean you've not consciously tuned in to this child. No child should be "un-noteworthy" for several weeks! This child is typically one of the good little boys and girls, neither struggling nor excelling, but compliantly and steadily journeying along through kindergarten. Chances are, you've not focused a lot on this child, since he or she has not demanded your attention in any unusual way. Challenge yourself to find something notable about this child over the next few days.

Parent Input: Listening for the Important Stuff

Getting parent input as early in the year as possible pays big dividends for the student, the teacher, and the family. The parent knows the child better than we can ever hope to know the child. True, parent assessment of behavior and personality is often emotionally charged, but we need to hear the parent's perspective and sort out those things that we know will be important in the classroom. (Mom says, "Reggie is very, very shy, but once he warms up, you'll find out he already knows letters and sounds." Based on this, you might delay doing early pretesting of letters and sounds for a week or two.)

Parent input is valuable in building background on each child's strengths and needs, and kindergarten is a wonderful opportunity to begin convincing parents that school is a partnership between teacher and family. After all, no matter how effective our instruction, children learn first and most powerfully from their families. In creating profiles for your children, it makes sense to ask parents what they have observed about their child's learning patterns, interests, and strengths. You may want to start the year by asking your students' families to fill out a parent survey, such as Markova's in *How Your Child Is Smart* (1992) or one that you've designed like the questionnaire below. Make sure that your survey allows parents to tell you candidly what they want you to know about their child.

Kindergarten Questionnaire

Child's name_____

My child likes to be called _____

Dear Kindergarten Families,

You and I have the same goal for your child: an enriching year that builds solid skills for reading, writing, and math. But more importantly, you and I both want your youngster to develop self-confidence and a love of learning. To accomplish these goals, I am asking you to help me get to know your child better. Any insights you can share with me will help me tailor my instruction to better serve your young learner. Please use this informal survey to clue me in to what makes your child tick! Answer only those questions for which you are comfortable sharing information with me. Use the back of this sheet or extra sheets if necessary. This survey will not become part of your child's permanent record file, and it will only be used by me to learn some of what you already know about your little scholar!

1. How do you describe your child's personality?
2. Tell me about any special interests, hobbies, or talents your child has.
3. What are your child's favorite toys or playtime activities?
4. Who are your child's favorite playmates?
5. How much time does your child spend outside? What are his or her favorite outside activities?
6. Is your child involved in any organized group activities, such as story hour or peewee sports?
7. Is your child afraid of anything?
8. Are there siblings? How old? Do they get along?
9. Are there behavioral, health, or allergy issues you'd like me to know about?
10. Please tell me anything else you want me to know about your little one.

Remember, you are your child's first, best, and most important teacher! Let your child know that you are interested in what is going on at school. Your attitude, your expectation of success, and your support will determine your child's approach to school. You and I are partners in learning!

Sincerely,

As the parent surveys are returned, spend some time with each. Use a highlighter to note those comments that are particularly enlightening or curious. Use what you learn to initiate conversations with shy children. ("Tell me about that tree house your Dad said you built in the woods.") Making a specific, personal reference to something in the child's world lets the child know you care. When a child seemingly has no idea what to write about or picture-write in his journal, remind him or her of a special playmate or favorite outside game. Let the child know that Mom or Dad told you, "right here on this paper that you go to gymnastics on Thursdays!" Knowing that Marcus has a passionate interest in farms will have you checking for farm books, brochures, and magazines that you can add to your Book Nook.

Of course, you won't carry all information about all children in your head. Save these parent surveys in your informal file, and reread each at least once each quarter and always before conferring with a family. Parent comments that seem unremarkable in early September may shed light on an incident in December. ("Oh, I see why LaToya is so emotional about Terence moving away. Her best friend in her apartment building moved last summer. Mom wrote it was traumatic for LaToya.")

We depend on parents to help us build a background of understanding about their child. In a differentiated classroom, much of what a parent tells the teacher can be used to help plan instruction and strategy.

Call or otherwise contact a few parents a week during the first month of school, even if you have met them before school started. Once the children begin to settle into a routine, initiate a casual, friendly conversation with a parent. Ask:

"What is Jonah saying about school?"

"Has Jonah mentioned anything he really likes at school? Any special friends?"

"From your perspective as a parent, how do you feel he is settling in? Does he seem to have any fears or concerns? Do you have any?"

Parent conferences are important, but impromptu, five-minute conversations with a parent *at any time* during the school year;

they will help you learn about the children in your class and will have even more far-reaching benefits. Open the conversation by asking the parents how they see things based on what they are hearing from their youngster. Consult parents often and acknowledge that they are their child's first, best, and most powerful teachers. These informal chats create mutual respect, make you and the school appear approachable, and give clarity to the child: "Wow, my teacher talks to my dad!" During, or as soon as possible after a conversation, jot notes to add to your informal profile.

How much parent input? How often? When?

Chances are that your school administration has a predetermined conferencing schedule in place. You may be required or encouraged to conference once each quarter or once each semester. Effective times to conference for children with no serious concerns are:

- a few weeks into the year;

- after the first marking period;

- several weeks before the end of the year; and

- whenever a parent requests to meet.

You will need to conference with some parents monthly or bimonthly if:

- there is little progress or no progress in academic skills;

- behavior is out of control; or

- you see a need for other professionals (school psychologist, occupational therapist) to become involved in the child's instruction.

Not all parents are eager to meet with you; don't take it personally. Some are overwhelmed with the stresses of everyday life; some are unavailable during school hours; some have no child-care for younger siblings; some have unpleasant memories of their own school experiences. Face-to-face conferences are best, but any communication is better than no communication. Ask if they have access to e-mail; if they have a telephone, ask what would be a convenient time to call; invite them to bring younger children. (Set out some toys that are safe for younger children.)

Give each child a folder (or include a two-pocket folder on your list of school supplies) to carry back and forth each day. The Home to School sheet (page 39), when run on brightly colored paper, is a simple, non-threatening way for you and the family to send quick messages back and forth. As this Home to School sheet becomes full, simply replace it with a new one. Save the old one to add to the child's profile.

Portfolio Assessment: "Look What I Did!"

Kindergarten teachers have been selecting and preserving samples of student work for as long as kindergarten children have been producing. A portfolio is a collection of student work samples, each labeled with a date. Teachers, students, and parents can look for individual growth and progress. The child's achievement is not measured by comparing work to others in the classroom, but by examining artwork, skill sheets, writing samples, and other evidence of the child's performance.

Some of the best work our kindergarten children produce cannot logistically become part of a portfolio. Clay models often need to be recycled so that someone else can use clay, patterns made from interlocking cubes need to be disassembled, and bridges creatively engineered from building blocks must come tumbling down. Often it is these very pieces that best represent a child's approach to learning, mastery of a skill, or cooperative work with others. In these cases, a photograph of the work will save it for the portfolio. One picture can be worth a thousand words!

What to include in the portfolio is largely up to you and the child. Of course you will save pieces that are representative of the child's strengths or weaknesses, but the child should also be allowed to add pieces that he or she is especially proud of. Let the children call it "My Best Work Folder," "My Showcase of Work," or "My Kindergarten Log of Learning." One Friday a month, you might say, "Boys and girls, look at your take-home folder that has all this week's papers for you to take home. Look through and take out two or three that you think show your best effort this week. Put them in the portfolio basket (or treasure basket or showcase basket). I'll check through and choose one to go in your portfolio." Reminding students frequently of your criteria for good work increases awareness of their own efforts.

You will be delighted to see the scrutiny that goes into this self-assessment process, especially if you have been coaching children in self-assessment often. Children begin to look at their work through more critical eyes: "I'll put this one in because it's really neat and colorful, but this other one looks a little scribbly." Or, "Hey, look, I want to use this one because none of my numbers are backwards on it!"

Home to School . . . and Back Again
A Quick Note to or From the Teacher

Dear Families,

This sheet should stay in your child's folder all month. If you need to ask a quick question or let me know something, jot it here. I check the folders every morning. Likewise, if I need to send you a comment, it will be here. Please initial, so that I know you have read it! (I'll do the same for you!)

Date	Comments, questions, concerns about _____ child's name	Initials

A Look Inside a Differentiated Classroom: Informal Assessment in Action

Thursday afternoon, 1:25: Ms. K comes back into her classroom after delivering her class to Mr. M, the primary music teacher. She's confident that today they'll especially enjoy their time with him. Last week she left him a note that she and the children are having fun making up nonsense rhyming words. Did he have any silly songs with nonsense rhyming that he could use with them in music class? If so, she would follow up by writing the silly words from songs he might teach them. Today he showed her the CD of silly songs he's chosen to use and gave her the lyrics to two songs they'll be learning and dancing to today.

Ms. K sighs heavily as she falls into her chair at her desk. Like every kindergarten day, today has been so busy that she's had no time to think. She takes a minute to straighten and organize her desk, and then she reaches into her apron pocket and brings out the small notebook with the colorful tabs that she carries all the time. The children call it Ms. K's journal because they often see her writing in it during their journal time, as well as at other times during the day. Occasionally, Ms. K stops a lesson, pulls out her notebook, and says, "Wow, boys, and girls! Before I forget, I have to write down, once again, that you folks are awesome learners!" Only Ms. K knows that she is writing "Brad: *the*—no wall."

That cryptic shorthand will remind her later that she saw Brad write the sight word the without running over to check the sight word wall as he usually does.

Tomorrow Ms. K will conference with Jared's family. She pulls out Jared's folder, not the official school guidance record that will follow him from classroom to classroom, school to school, but her own informal Jared collection, the one that contains "Jared" pages torn from her "journal" several weeks ago, as well as the Kindergarten Questionnaire completed by Jared's family early in the school year. Rereading the questionnaire allows Ms. K to see Jared through the eyes of the people who love him most (the questionnaire appears earlier in this chapter).

Ms. K sorts through her informal assessment notes (torn from her I-FAN) and decides which are relevant in reporting Jared's progress ("3/8 Crying...can't find the right sight word; 3/29 Asked Jenny for help; 4/17 Helped Brad find 'the' on wall"). She recalls the incidents that need discussing with Mom and Dad as behavior concerns ("3/8 Rough day. . . punched Kaley-hard!; 3/14 Stomped Toby— toe—hard! 4/14 Squeeze Alex from behind . . . A. hurt") and that trigger questions that she needs to ask Mom and Dad. ("3/22- says he's going to have his tonsils out?")

Next Ms. K looks through the work samples in Jared's portfolio. (More about portfolios later in this chapter.) She looks over the pieces added since the last report card was sent home. She will proudly be showing Jared's parent(s) how Jared's pencil and scissor control have improved. As she glances over other pieces, Ms. K realizes that Jared is no longer writing any numbers backwards. "Hooray! When did that happen?"

Ms. K begins writing out the parent conference comments, knowing that giving concrete examples is more effective than saying, "Jared is coming along in skills." Likewise, specific examples of misbehavior (without including the other child's name) give more clarity than saying, "Jared is having problems with his friends." She knows what she saw, but if she had not made notes, she would be hard-pressed to remember details.

Helping Children Self-Assess

In a differentiated classroom, children are encouraged to be aware of their own progress. Kindergarten teachers are excellent at acknowledging growth through nurturing comments ("Sasha, you're always remembering now to leave spaces between your words! Good for you!"). We need to consciously help children notice those things about their own work. Since kindergarten children are very concrete thinkers, they need to begin self-assessing by looking at individual samples of their own work. Zero in on specifics. These self-assessment strategies can be woven into your daily instruction:

- "Circle a word on your paper that would be easy for anyone to read."

- "Show your drawing to a friend and tell them what you like best about your work."

- "Is there one spot in your sentence that you could change to make it better?"

- "Put the face beside your name that matches how you think the name is written." (Page 45 shows a poster of faces that children can refer to regularly in evaluating their own work.)

When giving directions for a center, a skill sheet, or an activity, tell the children what you will be looking for in the finished product or during the process: "I need to see the pieces cut carefully, and no messy glue blobs!" or, "I'm looking for names neatly in the upper left, and every box with only one answer plainly circled," or, "I'm watching to see if you clean up your scraps from cutting before you assemble the scarecrow pieces and add the straw." Make your expectations concise and crystal clear, so that the child knows the standard that has been set. Knowing where the "goal line" is makes it easier for a child to see whether he fell short or scored.

A child's portfolio is an excellent means of convincing a young learner of his or her own progress. Children should be allowed to look through the collection of their work occasionally and encouraged to verbalize what they note as they compare work samples over several weeks. Ask children to do a self-portrait during the first week of school and write or dictate a sentence to you about themselves. Do the same activity mid-year, and let children compare the two. Save both, and repeat the activity near the year's end. How each child creates the self-portrait, describes him or herself, and prints any words along with the portrait will speak volumes about growth during the year.

When children are looking at two or three work samples spaced many weeks apart, give them clues to help them focus on the details:

- ■ "Do you see anything you got better at?"

- ■ "Look at how you wrote your name. Any differences?"

- ■ "Is there anything you think you know now that you didn't know before?"

- ■ "Is there anything that seems easy to you now that used to be hard to do?"

The busy kindergarten teacher rarely has time to individually conference with each child to compare his or her current work to previous work, although it is time well spent for students who still lack confidence. Once a marking period, pass out the current folders of work samples and allow children to sit with one or two friends. Since you have modeled the things you look for that show progress (such as the comments bulleted above), children will focus on the things that make their work "okay" or "good" or "my best!" Kindergarten children are very aware of what they *haven't* learned and *can't* do; they should be reminded regularly of what they *have* now learned and *can* now do.

How many work samples? Which ones? How often?

The portfolio should include representative writing samples, math practice sheets, center recording sheets, and drawings with and without scripted captions (written by student or teacher). Two or three samples per month that showcase literacy skills and an equal number that show math skills are sufficient to evaluate growth. Once a month, make a copy of a journal page from each child to include. Use photographs of a child doing center work, three-dimensional art projects, or playground fun to complement the paper-and-pencil samples.

A Look Inside a Differentiated Classroom: Coaching Self-Assessment

Thursday morning in Ms. K's classroom: The children are on the rug in front of Ms. K. Children are working with words that end in the rime -op. Together they come up with *hop* and *mop*, both of which have been written on the big chart by Ms. K's chair. Each child replicates the words on his or her own clipboard. Ms. K knows that using words aloud in sentences helps build comprehension and fluency for kindergarten children, so she stops for a moment.

"Before we go any further," Ms. K says, "we need to make sure we can use each word in a sentence. While I count to five, you each think of a sentence using one of these -op words. Then we'll share. Ready, think! [Quietly and slowly she counts to five.] Okay, take turns saying your sentence to someone sitting next to you. Listen carefully, because you know you may have to tell the rest of us your friend's sentence." Ms. K has learned that children listen more carefully when they know they will be asked to repeat someone else's words!

There is considerable chatter and giggling, and Ms. K overhears several sentences. "Who wants all of us to hear their friend's sentence?" she asks. Jacob begins waving his arm. Ms. K acknowledges him.

"Ms. K!" Jacob is about to burst. "You gotta hear Emaline's sentence! It's funny! She used both words in one sentence! She said, 'If you hop on a mop you're a witch!' She made a rhyme!"

"Boys and girls," says Ms. K with a smile, "turn to Emaline and say, 'You're so creative!' "

Everyone turns toward Emaline. In one happy, supportive voice, they say, "You're so creative!" Emaline beams.

Ms. K continues, "Now, friends, we'll have a thinking moment." Ms. K turns on her deep, announcer's voice, "Ladies and gentlemen, complete silence, please, while everyone silently thinks of more -op words. In your head, picture what each word looks like, and how each would be used in a sentence. Today, we'll think of real words only, no nonsense words."

For several seconds, there is complete silence. The children have used Thinking Moments before. They know the procedure. Ms. K breaks the silence.

"Okay. You've got your words, you've got your clipboards, make those -op words appear!"

The children begin to write on their clipboards. After a minute or two, Ms. K stops them. She asks each child to draw a line on his or her clipboard under the last word he or she wrote. With this cue, they can see how many words they themselves generated before they "put their heads together" as a class. Children add words from their clipboards to the list on the chart paper and then add words to their own clipboard lists from the chart. One at a time, someone uses each -op word in a sentence. Together, they spell each with emphasis on the -o and the -p, and even chant the spelling form. ("T-o-p— tall letter, short letter, below-the-line letter spells top!")

At the end of the lesson, Ms. K helps the children focus on their own papers. She directs the children to see details in their own work: "Look at your words. Think about the way you wrote your letters and how easy it would be for someone else to read what you wrote. Find the one word that you think you wrote most neatly and circle it. [She pauses while children study their work and circle their neatest word.] Now see if there is a word that you feel looks really messy or unreadable. If there is, put an 'x' through it. Only one 'x' allowed! [Again, she watches as they evaluate their papers.] Rewrite the word the way you *want* it to look. [Again, she gives them a moment.] Now, find an -op word that you really think is a fun word, or an interesting word, or a cool word. Put a dark rectangle around that word. When you go to the word center this week, at one point, you'll take your -op paper from your work folder. You'll have the chance to use your chosen word in a sentence and then illustrate the sentence. Or you might choose to use your word and other -op words in silly rhyming sentences, like the one Emaline gave."

How Do I Feel About How I Did?

I feel proud. I did my best.

I feel okay. I did all right.

I feel disappointed. I could do better.

Encourage children to self-assess by choosing a face to draw on their paper as they finish.

The children complete one more self-assessment before they put away their –op papers. Ms. K gives a directive that the children hear at least two or three times a week: "Find the face from the poster that tells how you feel about your work today, and draw that face at the top of your paper," she says. Many of the children immediately know which face to draw. Others reflect on their paper and glance at the wall where they see the poster titled, "How Do I Feel About How I Did?" In a few moments, each has drawn a face on his or her own paper.

Feedback From School Staff: Lots of Eyes and Ears

Feedback and input from other adults in the school can help you broaden your view. Yours are not the only eyes and ears tuned in to the child's life. Ask special area teachers, paraprofessionals, and others for their impressions. (Be sure to filter out the adult perception and interpretation of the behavior from the actual behavior.) These quick, informal conversations can occur at lunchtime, before or after school, or as you deliver and retrieve children from special area classes.

Formal Assessments: Another Piece of the Profile

Formal assessments (kindergarten screenings, standardized tests, and evaluations done for report cards) complement informal teacher and parent assessments and add another piece to the child's profile. Our informal, observational evaluations are nearly always confirmed by quantitative, formal assessments. Most often these assessment instruments are standard for all kindergartens in a given district or county. These formal evaluations and tests offer information on what a child knows and can be a credible piece of the profile, but they should not be the sole factor controlling an instructional plan or a placement decision.

How important is it to use formal assessments?

Kindergarten teachers intuitively recognize progress, perceive strengths and weaknesses, and sense who needs what. However, we must have concrete, measurable evidence of progress and skills, as well as documentation that supports decisions for instruction. Formal assessments such as checklists are easy for parents to understand and set realistic goals for teachers.

We build credibility when we present substantive evidence of our daily observations, and our record keeping should include both our informal and formal assessments. Furthermore, a documented paper trail is valuable (and required) for children who may have exceptional needs. Patterns of learning difficulties (or indications of giftedness) must be verified if we recommend those children for specific programs, such as special education or gifted and talented programs, that occur outside of the traditional classroom.

Kindergarten Screening: The First Step

Kindergarten screening as a measurement of school readiness is happening in more and more schools. Some schools screen before the first day of school; many screen during the first week or two. Most of the commercially available screening instruments assess a child's conceptual knowledge, fine- and gross-motor skills, and language skills, both receptive and expressive. The scaled scores are based on the child's chronological age at the time of the screening.

Although these standard screening instruments are valuable, they are not meant to indicate IQ or to predict school success. The intended use is to red-flag possible learning problems and to give a general assessment of readiness. If you choose to or are required to use a screening test, keep in mind that kindergarten screening is one important piece of the child's profile, but it is subject to so many

---

Some of the most common screening instruments for determining school readiness and/or developmental ages are:

- DIAL R and DIAL 3, authored by C. Mardell-Csunowski and D.S. Goldenberg (Developmental Indicators for Assessment of Learning, Revised Edition and Third Edition. 1990. American Guidance Services, a division of Pearson Educational Services, Upper Saddle River, NJ).

- ABC School Readiness Inventory by Normald Adair and G. Blesch (1996. M.D. Angus and Associates, Point Roberts, WA).

- Brigance Kindergarten Screening II by William Brigance (Curriculum Associates, North Billerica, MA).

- Child Development Inventories (CDI) by Harold Ireton, for parents and teachers (1992. Behavior Science Systems, Minneapolis, MN).

- Kaufman Survey of Early Academic and Language Skills (KSEALS) by Alan S. Kaufman and Nadeen Kaufmann (1993. American Guidance Services, a division of Pearson Educational Services, Upper Saddle River, NJ).

- Kindergarten Readiness Test (KRT) by Sue Larson and Gary Vitali (1988. Hawthorne Education Services, Columbia, MO).

variables that we must be cautious when we interpret results. These screening scores alone should not be touted as reliable indicators of skill levels or future achievement. Remember, formal testing is foreign and uncomfortable for many children, especially for children who are extremely shy and nonverbal, children who have had little contact with adults outside their immediate families, or children who are second-language learners. These youngsters may blossom once they feel safe and valued in a nurturing classroom, yet their "low" screening score may red-flag them, indicating that they are not ready for the kindergarten experience. Schools (especially public schools) screen children who are legally old enough to attend kindergarten, and no child is denied entry based on a screening score. In a perfect world, given time and resources, those children who appeared "unready" would be screened again once they have "warmed up" to school. Since that option is unlikely, a wise teacher looks at the screening through wary eyes and remembers that it is just that: a screening. A teacher working to differentiate her classroom will review and consider the screening results, but will conscientiously observe all children during the first few weeks of school to broaden her view and to confirm or question screening results.

All methods of assessment make errors: the errors made by formal tests are different from those made by informal or anecdotal record and documentation notes; the errors made by specific checklists of behavioral items are different from those made by holistic impressionistic assessments. Awareness of the potential errors of each evaluation or assessment strategy can help minimize errors in interpretation. It is a good idea to strive for a balance between global or holistic evaluation and detailed specific assessments of young children.

–Dr. Lilian Katz, A Developmental Approach to Assessment of Young Children, April 1997.

Academic Checklists: Assessing Skills and Concepts

The piece of the learner's profile that will most impact instructional planning will be the skill level of the child, especially in the crucial areas of literacy and math. In a differentiated kindergarten, skill assessment occurs *before, during,* and *after* specific skill instruction, through ongoing observational notes and samples of the child's work. We can't make logical decisions about instruction for a child unless we know where that child is on the skills continuum.

Formal, systematic literacy and math assessments are a regular component of most commercially prepared kindergarten reading and math programs. Your school, your district, or your county may require that these or other locally designed assessments be administered at specific intervals during the school year. These formal assessments are excellent for pinpointing mastery of skills, and the data should be an integral part of the child's profile. In a differentiated classroom, a teacher uses what she learns from formal assessments primarily to group children for reinforcement or for enrichment. Remember, however, that skill acquisition is dynamic, and skill needs are constantly changing for any child. Logically, then, groups need to be continuously changing, based on current needs of children. Likewise, the expectations on the assessments need to change over the course of the year. A January skills assessment would look different from one given in May.

Many valid, kindergarten-friendly assessments for math and reading exist. However, the perfect one for your classroom is the one that reflects your curriculum, themes, expectations, and instruction. The simplest guide to use in making your own skills checklist is the kindergarten report card that you use for informing parents of progress. That reporting tool lists the benchmarks for children as they travel through kindergarten. Use it as a tool that marks your targeted benchmarks for each marking period.

On pages 50 and 51 are literacy and math checklists of skills that I use as year-end goals. Children at the end of kindergarten in most states and provinces are expected to show mastery of these basic skills. Specific targets within the checklists can be adapted to reflect your specific expectations. For example, your school policy may ask that children know a specific number of sight words, or be able to count by rote to 20, not 30.

Classroom, district, and county expectations vary widely, depending on local policy. When designing a literacy and/or math checklist, it should reflect specific guidelines for your school. For example:

■ How many and which sight words are required?

■ Is there an expected reading level by the end of the year?

■ Which punctuation marks should be in use?

■ How far should a child be able to count?

■ How far is a child expected to be able to write numbers?

■ Which shapes need to be mastered?

■ To what sum should addition be performed?

■ Which coins must children recognize?

End-of-Year Kindergarten
Skills Checklist **Literacy**

Name_____ Date_____

Teacher _____

Concepts of Print: I know that print has meaning.

_____ I can handle a book correctly to find the front.

_____ I can point out the cover and the title of a book.

_____ I recognize some environmental print.

_____ I recognize _____ high-frequency sight words, from a list of _____.

_____ I can point out a letter, a word, and a sentence.

_____ I can follow text left to right, top to bottom.

Phonemic Awareness and Phonics: I can identify letters and sounds of spoken language.

_____ I can name _____ uppercase and _____ lowercase letters of the alphabet.

_____ I can point out specific letters in text.

_____ I can identify words with identical initial sounds.

_____ I can identify and create rhyming words.

_____ I can identify the sounds for _____ letters.

_____ I can fluently read consonant-vowel-consonant (CVC) words.

Comprehension: I understand that text has sequence and meaning.

_____ I can discuss what has been read to me.

_____ I can identify characters and events from a story.

_____ I can relate a story to a personal experience.

_____ I can retell a story.

_____ I can predict events in a story.

_____ I can sequence story events.

Writing: I understand that my thoughts can be communicated on paper.

_____ I can picture-write (draw) to convey meaning.

_____ I can dictate meaningful script for my picture writing.

_____ I can write letters to represent sounds.

_____ I use phonetic spelling to write words.

_____ I can correctly write high-frequency words.

_____ I use conventions of writing: capital letters.

_____ I use conventions of writing: spaces between words.

_____ I use conventions of writing: punctuation at the end of sentences.

End-of-Year Kindergarten
Skills Checklist **Math**

Name_____ Date_____

Teacher _____

Number Sense: I demonstrate a sense of numbers and sets.

_____ I can count by rote to _____.

_____ I recognize numbers through 20. (Numbers I do not recognize:_____)

_____ I can count sets of objects up to _____.

_____ I can form sets of a given number up to _____.

Communication: I can express ideas with math concepts.

_____ I can write numbers in sequence through _____.

_____ I can identify, draw, and describe a circle, triangle, square, and rectangle.

_____ I can identify and know the meaning of math symbols:

_____ a + sign means "plus."

_____ a − sign means "minus."

_____ an = sign means "is equal to."

_____ I use basic math vocabulary: less, more, larger, smaller, and so on.

Ordering, Sorting, and Using Reasoning and Proof: I understand the logic of mathematics.

_____ I can identify patterns.

_____ I can create a pattern.

_____ I can extend a variety of patterns.

_____ I can sort and classify, and can name common attributes in a collection.

_____ I can draw conclusions about relationships based on size or length.

_____ I know whether to add or subtract to solve simple word problems.

_____ I can find and justify answers to simple addition and subtraction using manipulatives.

Connections: I use math and math concepts to interpret the real world.

_____ I can use data to create a graph.

_____ I can interpret data from a graph.

_____ I can use nonstandard units of measurement.

_____ I can recognize and make reasonable estimations.

_____ I can recognize and name a penny, a nickel, and a dime.

_____ I can name the values of a penny, a nickel, and a dime.

Measurement, Time, and Money: I use the language of math.

_____ I understand the attributes of time, weight, length, and volume.

_____ I use numbers and comparisons in daily conversation.

Modalities Checklists: Noticing How They Learn

We know that kindergarten children are exploring all modalities and intelligences, but it is worthwhile to make some observations about those emerging preferences. (See Chapter 2 for details of modalities and intelligences.) Noticing a child's learning preferences, especially if one modality seems more obvious, adds an important dimension to his or her profile. If a child is struggling with a specific skill, you can tailor reinforcement and reteaching activities to engage the modality that appears to be comfortable for that child. ("Kenya is still not recognizing coins. I know how strongly visual she is. I'll get out the tracing paper and let her do coin rubbings, and I'll ask her to use the magnifying glass to find details on each. I think Tommy will enjoy that, too. He can use the practice! The rest of the class will love it, too. I'll set it up as a center.") Likewise, children ready for a challenge will be more likely to engage in an activity that is very comfortable for them. ("Audrey, Tanya, and Raoul love to listen and retell. I think they could prepare a skit for the rest of us based on 'Stone Soup.'")

You may want to include the Modalities of Learning Checklist (page 53) in each child's kindergarten profile. Before the end of the first marking period, complete a checklist for each child. Be aware of consistent behaviors or choices that begin to identify a child as a visual, auditory, or kinesthetic learner. Midway through the year, take another look. This time use ink of a different color to mark what you have noticed. Patterns may or may not become apparent. Keep in mind that five- and six-year-olds are still exploring modalities.

Ask parents to complete the same checklist based upon their observations. Share these observations with other adults who interact with the child. Occasional review of these checklists will help you keep individual children in mind as you design whole-group activities, sponge activities, and centers. (More in Chapters 4 and 5.) You may have Molly specifically in mind as you plan a very movement-rich whole-group activity, but rest assured that Molly is not the only child who will be enriched. Paying attention to *their* modalities of learning will assure that your lessons reflect more than just *your* modalities of learning.

How can I be sure I build an adequate profile for each child?

Relax! You don't have to know everything about every child. Don't drive yourself to the brink of insanity trying to profile each child in

Modalities of Learning Checklist

Child_____ **Date**_____

Check each description that applies to the child. Considerably more checks in one category may indicate an inclination toward that modality of learning. Remember: young children may show strengths in many modalities, or they may have not yet established a preferred modality.

A Visual Learner:

_____ Notices details in the room; notices when something has been moved or changed
_____ Watches intently when being shown how to do something
_____ Can remember where a picture or a word was on a page
_____ Studies posters, visual displays, and pictures
_____ Draws lots of details in pictures
_____ Recognizes people by face, physical characteristics, or clothing, but maybe not by name
_____ Loves to look at books
_____ Likes orderliness, tidiness
_____ Likes to sit in front to "see the pictures"
_____ Observes quietly those around him or her

An Auditory Learner:

_____ Listens well when being read to, even without seeing pictures
_____ Is always ready to talk
_____ May be easily distracted by sounds in the hall, outside the window, or in the classroom
_____ Uses a wide range of pitch, volume, and inflection in speaking
_____ Can follow three or more verbal instructions
_____ Talks to him- or herself
_____ Enjoys role-playing, skits, and dramatizations
_____ Shows interest in music, poetry, rhyming words, and phonemic awareness activities
_____ Counts out loud when working independently or reads aloud during silent reading time
_____ Uses words to express emotions: "I'm so happy!" "I'm really mad!"

A Kinesthetic/Tactile Learner:

_____ Likes to build, construct, and engineer things
_____ Sways, rocks, and moves with music
_____ Is well coordinated
_____ Strokes, touches, feels things
_____ Gestures a lot when talking
_____ Ends up messy, wrinkled, and disheveled from lots of movement
_____ Grips pencils and crayons with firm, if not accurate, grip
_____ Enjoys athletics, dance, gymnastics
_____ Shows emotions physically by hugging, clapping, jumping
_____ Likes action and adventure books

detail. Some checklists and charts will subdivide learning modalities, ask you to distinguish between modality and learning styles, or encourage you to identify secondary intelligences and talents. For in-depth behavioral and psychological evaluations, and for strategies to deal with learning disabilities, those tools are helpful. For a kindergarten teacher seeking to give every child the best possible opportunity to succeed, such complex assessments will only serve to frustrate the teacher and ultimately take a lot of time away from planning the *real* business of teaching.

When a teacher spends energy learning all he or she can about each child, each will show growth and experience success. In the care of a committed, perceptive, knowledgeable teacher, any curriculum, any unit, any lesson can lead children to successful learning. Chapter 4 will help you begin to "walk the walk" by preparing your students, yourself, and your instruction for a differentiated classroom in which each child feels like an important, competent discoverer.

Chapter 4

Setting the Stage for Differentiating

To be successful in differentiating your classroom, you must personally believe that not all children will learn best by doing exactly the same activity at exactly the same time as all other children. Once you accept and become excited about the power of that concept, you must set the tone for the class to make differentiation part of your students' belief system, also. Since kindergarten children have limited experience in the world of traditional classrooms, they readily accept whatever you, the beloved teacher, believe and model. ("If Ms. K says it, it must be true!")

The Big Sell: It's Okay That We're Working on Different Things!

Even if you are well into the school year, you can begin to differentiate your kindergarten. Explain ahead of time that every child is responsible for his or her own learning, but that you are there to coach everyone. Tell them matter-of-factly that there will be times when some children will be doing one thing and some another, and that not all children will do all activities.

Most children can understand either of these analogies:

■ "When our school band plays, every musician has to focus on his or her own instrument. To become excellent at playing their instruments, some will do more finger exercises, some will do more breathing exercises, and others will have to practice reading music more than their friends. Just like musicians, we kindergartners all have some things in which we need more practice than do others. As your teacher, I am like the Band Leader, and I must help you practice in the ways that are best for you."

- "If you watched our high school soccer team at practice, you would see some players running to build up strength, some would be working on passing the ball smoothly, and some doing bending and stretching exercises. As your teacher, I am the coach who will help you be the best player you can be. I may ask you to do different things than some of your classmates are doing, because it's my job to help you do your very best!"

Build the Atmosphere of Differentiation Right From the Beginning

Let families know the power of your strategy and why yours is not a one-size-fits-all classroom. Building a relationship of mutual support between your classroom and the home will reinforce your program of differentiation, encourage families to celebrate their children's uniqueness, and ultimately allow children to blossom.

The letter on page 58 combines a message to families stating the goal of helping children appreciate personal strengths and differences with a simple request for data that will support a related class activity. Use this letter or one of your own to communicate your goal and collect information on early milestones (walking, talking, shoe-tying) to use in a class lesson on appreciating differences.

Once families have completed and returned the surveys (and you don't need all of them to accomplish your objective), you have the makings of several solid math lessons. You may also have material for modeled writing, shared writing, and interactive writing lessons, all of which can positively highlight children's differences. For example, you might want to prepare the completed graphs ahead of time, and let children come up with sentences that correctly interpret the data that they see. ("What can we say is true when we look at our graph called 'We All Learned to Talk'? Right! The graph shows that three of us were talking before we were 18 months old.") Continue to analyze the data and introduce math concepts of more than, less than, and equal to.

For a modeled or shared writing lesson that helps children build language skills around the graph, write the sentences that the class has generated. ("Ramon said, 'The most don't even know how to tie our shoes yet, like me.' Ramon, may I rearrange your words just a bit? Thanks. Let's write this: 'Most of us do not tie yet.' Does that say what you meant, Ramon? You bet it does. Let's write those words.") The children love the sentence-writing activity because all the data relate to their lives.

Or you may want to label only the columns, and let children use sticky colored dots to complete each task, as a hands-on introduction to graphing data. ("When I read the papers your parents filled out, I learned that five children in our class learned to tie a shoe after they turned four but before they turned five. Which column says that? Who can come and put a sticky dot in each of five boxes in that column?")

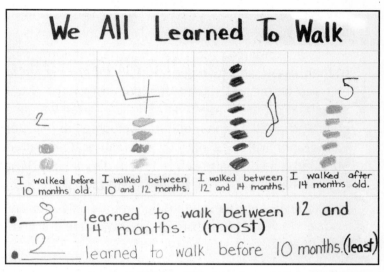

Use data gathered from "Early Milestones" parent input (page 58) to create graphs—proof positive that we all learn at different rates, but we all learn!

By creating and interpreting one graph per day over the course of three days, you have repeated opportunities to reinforce the concept that all children develop differently. Meanwhile, you are introducing graphing and data interpretation skills. (Be certain to make at least one a horizontal graph to show several ways to represent the data.)

After these graphs are complete, leave them displayed in the room for as long as possible. Make frequent references to the graphs as you reinforce the idea that everyone learns, grows, and succeeds at different rates. Read favorite kindergarten books such as *Leo the Late Bloomer* by Robert Kraus or *The Little Engine That Could* by Watty Piper, and revisit the graphs to emphasize the span of "blooming" in your classroom.

Also have the graphs on display for families to view at Open House or Parent Conference Day. Use the graphs to reassure families that as a teacher, you honor individual differences and believe that all children can succeed.

Dear Kindergarten Families,

Our children possess a variety of talents and learn at different rates—just as we adults do. Some children have arrived at school with mastery of letters and sounds. Some are just beginning to develop a desire to learn letters and sounds. Some still just want to play! Yet all are intelligent, capable children who *will* be reading for meaning as adults. In fact, as long as your child is steadily growing in skills and confidence, learning to love learning, and finding success along the way, we can rest assured that he or she is well on the way to literacy.

In our classroom, too, I want to help children discover their unique strengths and those of their peers, and to accept that we all grow according to our own timetables. To help children better understand this idea, we will be discussing how as toddlers we all learned to walk at different ages, yet by kindergarten we are all walking. Then we will make some graphs to highlight three of our developmental milestones: walking, speaking, and shoe-tying. (Our graphs will show data by ages rather than names, so you do not need to label the attached questionnaire with your child's name.) The children will see that what matters is that we have all mastered these important skills, not how quickly or at what age we did it!

You can help us validate our uniqueness. Please complete this survey and return it by Friday. We will use the information to create our graphs. Thank you for helping your child learn that "It's okay to be myself!"

Your partner in learning,

_____

EARLY MILESTONES

1. When did your child begin to walk?
_____ Before 10 months old
_____ Between 10 months and 12 months old
_____ Between 12 months and 15 months old
_____ After 15 months old

2. When did your child begin to talk in phrases or sentences?
_____ Before 18 months old
_____ Between 18 months and 24 months old
_____ Between 24 and 30 months old
_____ After 30 months old

3. When did your child master shoe-tying?
_____ Before four years old
_____ Between four years and five years old
_____ After five years old
_____ Not yet

Everyone's on Board! What's Next?

Strategies for differentiation can be used for independent work time, whole-group instruction, centers, the physical setup of your classroom, and even the school supplies available for the children's use. In this section, we will explore successful routines and procedures that allow you to use independent work time to focus on one or two children at a time, zeroing in on the skills appropriate for modeling for each child at that moment. We'll deal with the challenges of teaching children to become self-managing. On page 72, we will take "A Look Inside a Differentiated Classroom" where independent work time is orderly, engaging for all children, and used for spontaneous teaching moments. Chapter 5 will give you strategies for differentiating instruction for the whole group and in centers, as well as tips and tools for setting up a supportive classroom environment.

Teaching Children to Manage Themselves

Children in a differentiated classroom learn to be very self-directed. This takes practice, routine, and monitoring. Certainly the earlier in the year children learn self-management, the earlier you can begin to differentiate. However, kindergarten children are very adaptable, and even in February they get excited when their teacher announces, "Boys and girls, you have grown up so much in the last few weeks, I think it's time you started making some decisions and choices for yourself, and solve some problems on your own!" Most kindergarten children will proudly rise to the reasonable expectations you have for them, provided you have given them the tools to use for self-help.

Children need established procedures to know what to do when they finish a task early. By refining, expanding, and balancing the choices you offer, you can easily provide differentiated learning options for the children, free yourself up to grab teachable one-on-one moments, and eliminate busywork that merely engages a child for the sake of keeping him occupied.

Teacher Is Not the Only Help in the Room: Self-Help Strategies

In a differentiated kindergarten, the teacher is often working one-on-one with a child or a small group of children for two to three minutes. Almost always, another child will need your help, and kindergarten children are not always skilled at waiting! By modeling self-help procedures early and often, you will be training the children to look to resources other than you for guidance.

Where in the room can I find help? Train the children to check the room for help. For example, make it a habit during shared or interactive writing to refer to the alphabet chart: "Hmm, I need to write the /f/ sound at the end of this word. Let's see if the alphabet chart can help. /f/, /f/. Oh, I see the picture that begins with that sound. What is it, boys and girls? Yes! It's the /f/, /f/, frog. What letter do you see by the frog? Right, again! It's an *f*. If I couldn't remember how to make it, I could always find the clues I need from the alphabet chart." In very similar ways, point out regularly the hundreds chart for writing numbers or the color words posted on the wall for reading and writing color words.

Make it a point to think aloud often in order to model how to find help from classroom resources. "Could the word wall of high-frequency words help someone who is stuck with writing? Do we have a list of weather words you could consult when you need one? Is there a friend who could help?" Train your learners to be detectives! I often prompt students with a challenge: "Where in the room could you get the answer to that without asking? Learning detectives know how to use the clues!"

Do I already know how to handle this? In addition to finding academic answers around the room, teach your children the procedures for satisfying these other common needs:

- "I lost my yellow crayon!" All children know where the scrap crayon box is in which they can deposit found crayons or help themselves to one they need.

- "My pencil broke!" Since sharpening their own pencils can become a hobby for some children (especially those with a short attention span and a kinesthetic learning style) teach children to deposit their broken pencils in the ER (emergency room) Pencil Can to be sharpened later. They can take a "loaner" from the basket of sharpened pencils beside the ER can. At the end of the day, you or a student helper can sharpen those pencils.

- "I have to go to the bathroom!" Your procedure for bathroom and drinks will depend upon your individual situation. If the bathroom is in the classroom, it is simple to allow bathroom use during independent time. If the bathroom is several hallways away, you may need to depend upon classroom aides, older student helpers, or learned bladder control.

■ "Where are the brass fasteners for this project?" Have a shelf, table, countertop, empty desk, or other designated area where you always put the materials necessary for any independent project. Once you've modeled the procedure, children automatically know where to look to find brass fasteners, pipe cleaners, feathers, google eyes, wallpaper scraps, or any other novelty item pertinent to a project.

I'll find a friend who can help! Make certain your learners also feel comfortable asking one another for help. Encourage them to be "first aid for learning" for one another when you are busy. Start early in the year to build the "peers as coaches" attitude. For example:

"Jenny, I know you can zip a jacket. Please be our zipper coach today. Anyone who needs help zipping, line up in front of Jenny."

"Randy, Jack is pointing to the upper left on his paper. He'll help you find the upper left on yours."

"Look around your table and make sure all your friends have five frogs on their mats. Help each other count them out."

"You don't know what step comes next? Ask a friend who was listening."

Give children a visual clue that, unless they are "bloody, sick, or on fire," they must wait or find their own help. Use distinct, unmistakable cues.

■ "Whenever I have on this hat, it means, 'No interruptions, please.'"

■ "Whenever I have this COACH necklace around my neck, it means, 'No interruptions, please.'"

■ "Whenever I am at this table with the stop sign up, it means, 'No interruptions, please.'"

I can sign up for help! Teach children to exhaust the self-help possibilities before asking for your help. Designate a spot on a clipboard, chalkboard, or dry-erase board where children can sign up for your help after they have asked at least two friends. Or use a pocket chart in which children can put their own name card if they are stuck and need your help. One glance tells you who is waiting.

Providing Sponge Activities . . . Not Just "Fluff and Fillers!"

Give children well-defined choices of sponge activities to choose from when they are waiting for you or have finished an assigned activity. A sponge activity is a purposeful, self-selected activity that a child can quietly and independently choose if he has finished a task or is waiting for you to meet with him about his assigned task.

Choice changes the chemistry of the brain. When learners get to choose a task, the resources, or the parameters for accomplishment, their stress is lower. This triggers the release of our own 'optimal thinking' brain chemicals.

Allow your learners to continually make appropriate choices in their learning. The amount of choice offered should vary and be age-appropriate. Too much choice and the learners will only do things they are familiar with. Too little, and they'll never get to develop a passion for learning."

—ERIC JENSEN, *BRAIN COMPATIBLE STRATEGIES*, 1997

The term "sponge" was originally used by Madeline Hunter (1994) to describe an activity that turns potentially wasted time into productive learning time, reinforcing her belief that there should be no wasted moments in a classroom. Unfortunately, for teachers not familiar with Hunter's model and intent, sponge activities have become for some simply a way to fill time, with no learning objective attached. In a differentiated classroom, each sponge activity reinforces a concept already presented, provides practice in a target skill, and allows for exploration of varying modalities and intelligences.

Introduce sponge activities one or two at a time during the early days of the school year, or as soon as you begin to consciously differentiate. Think of these open-ended activities as anchor tasks, brain exercise, free-choice centers, or leisure learning, but always keep learning in mind. Although there are many times during the day when you are directing a child's learning, there must also be time for children to choose an activity. Meaningful sponge activities are a kid-friendly way to provide learning choices and opportunities in a differentiated classroom.

Sponge Activities as Learning Centers

Sponge activities are often games and manipulatives that will double as a Learning Center at another time during the year. In Chapter 5, you will see many of the sponge activities reappear as centers designed to follow up specific lessons with independent practice, reinforce key instructional objectives, or provide practice for targeted skills. As centers, they may be an assigned activity with corresponding recording sheets that assesses student understanding (see examples in chapter 5). Because the goal is for all students to complete the center work, these activities will often not be available as free-choice sponge activities.

Dominoes are a good example of a sponge activity that may be a math center later in the year. As a free-choice sponge activity, children are encouraged to explore with the dominoes by matching, building, and counting. Later, it becomes a center where the children will complete specific tasks. ("Close your eyes and take a domino from the pile. Count the number of dots on one side and write it in the left box on your paper domino. Now count the dots on the other end of the domino and write the number on the right side.") Because the children have already played with dominoes earlier in the year as sponge activities, they are ready for more structured use.

Free-choice sponge activities invite children to choose appropriate ways to interact with the materials. Objectives may differ for each child, but all are purposefully chosen to build readiness and enthusiasm for learning. When setting up an activity as a center, the teacher dictates the procedure for interaction with a specific instructional objective in mind. In contrast, sponge activities allow plenty of free exploration, an important prerequisite for use of any manipulative.

Free exploration does not imply, however, that no guidelines exist for the use of materials. The appropriate use of materials, as well as expectations for cleaning up, needs to be clear and consistent. Model how to handle materials, and discuss acceptable (and unacceptable) ways to interact with them. "A Look Inside a Differentiated Classroom" (pages 64 and 65) shows how well-managed sponge activities provide smooth transitions and meaningful work for children in between lessons.

How Do I Plan for and Manage Sponge Activities?

Sponge activities need to be easy to access and easy to clean up. They can be arranged at a designated table or can be portable in a tub, basket, or tote bag.

Think about the free-time choices in which your children may currently engage within your classroom. Now look at them from a differentiated point of view. Are you offering a variety of visual, spatial, and auditory selections? Are they easy to access and easy to put away? Are some activities meant to be done alone, while others present opportunities for cooperative effort? Are most open-ended so that a child could work with the materials for two minutes or ten? Do you rotate activities on and off the shelf so that there is often something new, or an old favorite has reappeared?

You will recognize most materials in the sponge activities described here as standard kindergarten supplies, toys, and games. While considered toys or "fun stuff" by the children, these items can be structured to become valuable tools to extend learning, practice fine-motor skills, build confidence, and allow children to explore many modalities and intelligences.

A Look Inside a Differentiated Classroom

It is 1:30 in Ms. K's Kindergarten. A few minutes ago, all children were gathered with Ms. K on the rug, talking about the delightful book they had just read: *Owly* by Mike Thaler. This book complements the theme she has been teaching: nocturnal animals. Earlier in the week, she had read both fiction and nonfiction books about raccoons, bats, moths, and other nocturnal animals.

Ms. K has shown the children tracers for owl heads, wings, and bodies; for cat bodies and tails; for moth body and wings; and for bat body and wings. Every piece that could belong to a bat is stamped with a bat stamp; every piece that could be traced for an owl is stamped with an owl stamp. In this way, children can figure out independently which pattern pieces they need.

Ms. K also knows that some of her very artistic children can draw a better owl, bat, moth, or cat than the tracers show. Therefore, she always tells the children that they do not have to use a tracer.

Now Ms. K has shown art materials and has modeled the procedure the children will use to make animals for their "Creatures of the Night" bulletin board. Each child will choose a night animal to make. It does not have to be one of the animals represented by the tracers that have been provided. Children may create any animal, as long as it is nocturnal. Children have returned to tables to begin making their animals. Some have chosen to use the tracers Ms. K has provided; others have started by drawing their own night animal.

Now Ms. K is circulating as the children work. Some design, cut, or attach feathers, wiggly eyes, and brass fasteners to create a head that turns to make an owl. She is stopping at each table to ask children to recall events, sequences, or descriptions from the story of Owly, or to encourage children to talk about the similarities and differences among the various night animals. At each table, her questions initiate conversation among the children. Ms. K knows that talking about stories is an efficient way to help build comprehension.

"Because the sun came up," says William when Ms. K asks the children at his table why Owly quit counting the stars in the sky. "He couldn't see them anymore."

"I think it wasn't a foggy night when Owly went out," offers Anna, working on her owl next to William. "Because if it was foggy he couldn't see any stars even if it's dark enough."

As William, Anna, and others at their table work and discuss the best time to view stars, Ms. K moves on to another table. She notices that Devon is on the floor with a sponge activity, working on an owl puzzle. His work station is cleaned up and a quick glance at the project counter (where children have been trained to put finished products) tells her that his owl is done.

As Gary finishes, he checks to see that his name is on the owl; cleans up his spot; puts scraps into the recycling box; puts his crayon box, scissors and glue back on the shelf (on his assigned number); and looks around the room. He (and the rest of the class) has practiced the cleanup procedure so many times that it has become automatic. Now he moves purposefully toward the shelf of portable sponge activities, chooses the magnetic shapes and the magnet board, and takes it back to his spot, where he chats with tablemates as he creates a skyscraper out of magnet pieces.

Soon most of the children are scattered around the room, all interacting with self-selected sponge activities. Ms. K moves over to Corey, a quiet little fellow in the Book Nook who often resists moving from one activity to the next. "Corey," she whispers. "The cleanup song is coming in two minutes. You'll have time to finish looking at this page, but then these books must go back on the shelf. Be listening for the signal!" Corey looks up at her with disappointment, but she reinforces the time by showing him two fingers. With a smile, she repeats, "Two minutes, champ!"

Ms. K moves toward Thomas and Quincy who are still working on owls. "Boys, put your brass fasteners into your crayon boxes, and your owls in the Catch-Up Cupboard. You'll need to finish these before you can start your centers this afternoon."

Ms. K takes a child-size xylophone from the file near her desk and runs the stick across the bars. Everyone stops and looks at her. She breaks into song, a cleanup ditty that the children recognize immediately. Most of them sing along with her:

(to the tune of "It's Howdy Doody Time")

"And now it's cleanup time,

it's happy cleanup time,

Put all your things away.

We'll get on with our day!"

The children sing along as everyone puts away sponge activities and moves toward the rug. (Some more eagerly than others!) Soon all are sitting cross-legged on the rug. Ms. K is in her chair, ready to address the whole group.

These sponge activities are a sampling of developmentally appropriate independent choices in a differentiated kindergarten. Each nurtures, supports, or appeals specifically to one or more of the multiple intelligences described in Chapter 2.

Tip!

No need to waste time trying to match lost puzzle pieces to the correct box. Code the back of each puzzle piece with a specific color, letter, number, or design for that puzzle.

An easy way to accomplish this with larger puzzles is to have the puzzle completed on a tray. Cover the completed puzzle with a piece of cardboard (pizza box or corrugated cardboard) and carefully invert the completed puzzle. Now color the back or code the back of each piece with a symbol before you disassemble the puzzle. If puzzles get mixed together, or if pieces are found a week later under the rabbit cage, the coding allows children to sort and to match lost pieces to the correct puzzle.

Sponge 1

Puzzles: Use puzzles with all levels of difficulty, and those that will appeal to a wide range of interests. Strongly visual-spatial children love complex jigsaw puzzles. Some children will be drawn to puzzles of Disney movies, while others prefer alphabet or number challenges. Let children begin assembly on a tray large enough for the entire puzzle, and make it an ongoing team effort. Tell children that when they must stop before finishing a puzzle, they should lay the completed sections on top of that frame so that the next puzzler can continue to work on it. Build your puzzle collection by asking parents for discards or by visiting yard sales and flea markets. The more puzzles you have, the more children you will engage, and the more often you can change the ones available at any given time.

Modalities and Intelligences: Puzzles develop visual-spatial intelligence, and appeal especially to visual and kinesthetic-tactile learners. Most children will want to see the box cover or completed puzzle first, but a child with strong visual-spatial skills may dump a 100-piece puzzle, toss the cover face down, and vigorously begin assembling with success. Even children who struggle with the fine-motor and eye-hand skills necessary for puzzle assembly will attempt and enjoy high-interest, wooden-framed puzzles, which usually have fewer pieces and have the pieces outlined on the frame as a guide.

Sponge 2

Listening Center: Children can easily learn to operate headphones and a tape player. If possible, have two tape players, each with two or three headphones attached to allow children at the same center to choose to listen to different things. Besides listening to books on tape, let children choose from music tapes (great for auditory learners or children with musical intelligence) or tapes of stories without accompanying books (terrific for developing visual comprehension—the ability to form a picture in your head.) Well-loved tapes that you use regularly (in my classroom these include Dr. Jean Feldman's *Sing to Learn* and Sharon MacDonald's *Jingle In My Pocket: Songs That Teach*) become popular choices and continue to teach during sponge-activity time. In addition to the standard storybooks on tape, put out nonfiction books. For example, during an insects unit, make a tape of yourself (or a parent or older student) reading a book about insects that is not on tape. Create similar tapes for many of the nonfiction books you use within themes or units to meet science and social studies standards. The children will choose from the tapes you have assembled, all of which will support classroom learning.

Modalities and Intelligences: The listening center appeals to and encourages auditory learning and intrapersonal intelligence, as a child can revel in his or her own little world, responding to the music or text in his or her earphones. Rotate the tapes regularly, but always offer a variety to stimulate musical, verbal-linguistic, and natural intelligences. Or offer a move-and-do tape (songs with finger or arm movements) for kinesthetic learning. Since this can be distracting to the rest of the room, consider putting the listening center behind a screen or other room divider.

Sponge 3

The Exploration Station: Nearly all children have an intense curiosity about the natural world around them. (Some experts feel that our natural intelligence is one of the first that we consciously develop.) Designate one or more areas of your room as the exploration station(s). This area could be a table, a shelf, a countertop, or a box that can be carried to a table. Leave magnifying glasses and something to observe and touch. Set rules from the beginning about methods for handling materials, acceptable voice levels for children discussing observations, and clean-up necessary for the activity. Science posters and supporting nonfiction books at this table help make important science connections.

Modalities and Intelligences: The exploration station allows hands-on, sensory investigation. Because the activity encourages children to touch, see, and discuss with their friends, they employ all modalities of learning. Depending upon the material at the table, children will access natural, visual-spatial, interpersonal, and logical-mathematical intelligences.

The Exploration Station: Ideas for Fun and Learning

■ Monarch caterpillars in a covered aquarium. This creature, which chews its way through milkweed, becomes a chrysalis, and emerges as a butterfly, provides a favorite late-summer sponge activity. Children learn about metamorphosis in a wonder-filled way.

■ A tray of regional flowers for children to dissect. This early experience with stems, leaves, petals, pistils, and stamens will lay groundwork for later plant units.

■ A sunflower head with tweezers provided for the children to remove the seeds. (Have a receptacle for the seeds. Use them later for estimating, breaking apart for science investigations, or gluing on art projects.) This activity strengthens fine-motor skills and sharpens observation.

■ An aquarium with magnifying glasses. Children will notice minute details on fish, tadpoles, and water plants.

■ A box full of autumn leaves, collected by the children if possible. Provide tracing paper and unwrapped crayons for rubbings

■ A tray of magnets of different strengths and shapes with a basket of items that will or will not be attracted to a magnet. Children will discover some basic laws of physical science.

■ Fossils with magnifying glasses. Children can share their creative guesses about what the creatures looked like and where the fossils were found.

■ An array of kaleidoscopes and prisms. Children will observe changing symmetry.

■ An ant farm (or two). Once again, a magnifying glass or two will keep children focused.

■ Boxes of seashells. Put out empty egg cartons and watch children begin to sort and classify.

Children practice classification and sorting skills as they discover seashells with similar shapes, patterns, and textures.

Clay Working: Working with clay is another popular sponge activity. When stored in a lidded, plastic box, clay can be used indefinitely. A child can take the box and a small tray to his or her spot to sculpt. By rolling, kneading, and shaping clay on the tray, the child has a defined workspace and also keeps oily, sticky residue off table surfaces. Children need to know that as a sponge activity, the clay models are temporary, and must be kneaded back into a ball for the next person to use, unlike the clay "assignments" in which finished products are for display. (See Chapter 5 for how to use clay in a learning center.) Knead in a few drops of scented oil or flavoring extract (see play dough recipe below) to add another sensory dimension. Having baby wipes available in the room makes finger clean up easy. (Note: Clay is a nasty culprit in harboring and passing germs. A good health habit is to have children use a baby wipe or the sink to clean their own hands before and after clay use.)

Modalities and Intelligences: Working with clay is a very sensory experience, and stimulates tactile learning. Clay also is a creative medium for visual-spatial learners, many of whom have budding artistic talent. Children with well-developed verbal-linguistic and interpersonal intelligences will verbalize entire scenarios for their friends as they make simple bird nests or animals. Those with intrapersonal intelligence may simply knead, roll, and shape the clay while reflecting on their own thoughts.

SCENTED PLAY DOUGH

1 cup salt
2 cups flour
1 Tbsp. cream of tartar
3 Tbsp. oil
2 cups boiling water
2 packages unsweetened powdered drink mix

Mix dry ingredients. Add oil. In a separate bowl, mix powdered drink mix and boiling water. Add to dry ingredients. When cool, knead until smooth. Store in airtight container, as mixture will dry and crack if left exposed. Make several different colors and flavors. Each will have a distinctive smell. Send the recipe home. Ask different parents to occasionally make a fresh batch to send to school.

Sponge 5

Book Nook: For optimal use, your classroom library areas must be attractive and comfortable. Consider big pillows on the floor, and beanbag or kid-sized chairs. Do you have a place for a floor lamp or table lamp to add a cozy touch? In addition to colorful and well-loved children's books, add several baskets for magazines, brochures, and advertising flyers. Display books and magazines that relate to any current classroom themes. Reluctant readers will often become excited over hunting flyers, race car magazines, travel brochures, farm catalogs, recipe books with pictures, heavy-equipment flyers, collector magazines, or atlases. Ask parents and colleagues for discarded hobby magazines. Stop at area motorcycle, ATV, scooter, or snowmobile stores, hobby shops, or farm implement dealers and ask for advertising brochures.

Modalities and Intelligences: A well-chosen variety of books will appeal to all learning styles. Visual learners love bright, distinctive pictures; tactile and kinesthetic learners are drawn to books that have pop-out features or textured pages; auditory learners love previously read predictable texts that they can read aloud. Children with verbal-linguistic intelligence will make up stories for the pictures, and those with logical-mathematical and visual-spatial intelligences will seek out books that invite them to find the object that doesn't belong or to locate a detail in a busy scene. Your musically intelligent children will rap and chant as they reread favorite sing-songy books you've read aloud.

> ■ **Tip!**
>
> No matter how much you practice and model reading to yourself with a soft voice, many kindergartners have difficulty using whisper voices. Cut the wires off old, worn-out headphones from outdated listening centers. Leave them in a basket near the Book Nook. Children who are distracted by others' reading can put on a set to block out distractions.

Sponge 6

The Publishing Spot: An open-ended art center, doubling as a message or writing center, is a favorite place to create for some children. (Think visual learners. Think visual-spatial intelligence. Think artistic talent.) Equip the area with standard art fare: crayons, markers, scissors, glue, and various papers including wallpaper, graph paper, old worksheets, and paper headed for recycling. Children will draw, color, cut, glue, and write. Ask parents to send you unused return envelopes (the kind that come in junk-mail offers). Children can seal and address notes for hand-delivery to friends and family.

Since their work here is often not open-ended, and since many children will feel the need to finish what they have started, provide a Catch-Up Cupboard or shelf nearby where children can leave the treasures they want to continue to work on at another independent work time. When you ask them to clean up sponge activities, make sure their names are on their projects, and deposit the projects in the Catch-Up Cupboard for safekeeping.

Once a week, announce that you'll be cleaning out the Catch-Up Cupboard, so if someone has an unfinished piece that is important to them, they need to complete it or take it home as is. (Most children, at the moment of cleanup time, ardently declare that they will finish this masterpiece. In reality, a few hours later they forget!)

The Catch-Up Cupboard gives children convenient storage for projects they'd like to (or must) finish.

Modalities and Intelligences: Publishing writing in different formats appeals to visual and tactile learners. Children exploring logical-mathematical intelligence may draw patterns; those exploring natural intelligence may draw intricate, detailed animals; those exploring verbal-linguistic intelligence may begin to write notes to you or each other or to add their own text to their drawings; still other children exploring intrapersonal intelligence may create "pictures I have in my head." For all children, the Publishing Spot encourages visual-spatial intelligence as they plan, organize, and create.

More Sponge Activities

Look around your room. Anything that can be done independently without distracting others can become a sponge activity. Sketching and viewfinder toys, memory games, building blocks and other manipulatives, and a host of other favorites can be much more than busy work. Make sure the activity meets these criteria:

- appeals to a variety of learning styles and intelligences

- can be used by learners of any skill level

- strengthens eye-hand development

- allows children to discover on their own ("Wow, this magnet can hold ten paper clips but only touches the first one!")

- encourages creativity

■ motivates children to discuss concepts ("The dinosaur in my puzzle was a meat-eater. Look at his sharp teeth.")

Most important for the success of the activity is that children are prepared to do it properly. As you introduce each sponge activity, model, model, model! Children need to be responsible for clean-up and storage. Make expectations specific and clear, and enforce them consistently. Introduce these activities two or three at a time and let children learn the rules as they interact with the materials. By providing a wide range of choices, you can engage students of all modalities and intelligences in what they consider fun and what you know is learning.

One of the goals of a differentiated classroom is to have no wasted instructional time. By guiding your children to self-manage sponge activities, you build in valuable and developmentally appropriate learning during the times when they would be waiting for others to finish a task or waiting for you to check their work.

Differentiating Lessons: Start Small for Success

Once you have cultivated classroom attitudes that allow students to focus on what they are doing rather than what others are doing; once children have become confident with self-help procedures; and once you have established routines for sponge activities, you can begin to differentiate instruction within a small block of time.

To plan a differentiated lesson, choose a concept that can be presented in several ways or a skill that can be practiced through different techniques. Your plan should take into consideration all of the following:

■ What is the goal of this lesson? What concept or skill am I teaching?

■ How can I effectively divide the class into three groups? (Social interaction should be a more important factor in your decision than ability or learning style.)

■ How will I structure the whole-group lesson to give the background the children will need?

■ What follow-up activity will be a largely auditory activity? Visual activity? Kinesthetic activity?

■ How can I clearly explain the procedure for each activity choice?

In this scenario, we'll assume you have done a read-aloud and whole group discussion of the folktale "Stone Soup." Your goal for the follow-up activity is to create a differentiated lesson that

a) provides children with different ways of responding to the literature, and

b) allows the opportunity to engage each child in a guided writing mini-lesson at the child's level.

By now, you've established expectations for work time, and children have regularly worked with sponge activities. You are ready to move into the differentiated lesson. Point out that at Table One you've left crayons, markers, colored pencils, and paper. Children working at this table will illustrate a scene from "Stone Soup." Later you will help them write a sentence or two to accompany their picture. If they finish, they should show their picture to a friend at Table One and practice saying the sentence they will want to write, or they can go get a story strip and begin to write their sentence! Or they can deposit their drawing (labeled with name!) in a designated basket, and do a sponge activity or a learning center until you are ready to help them with their sentence.

"Wait! What if I put a child in the wrong group, asking him or her to use a less-preferred learning style?" Don't panic! You cannot harm a child by having him or her work in any given modality—even if it isn't his or her best suit. In fact, it presents the child with an opportunity he or she might not have chosen. Remember, young children are exploring all modalities and exhibiting many over-lapping intelligences, and many kindergartners will not show clear evidence of any preference. And sometimes, just for the sake of evening out numbers, a random division of groups makes sense.

Next describe the task at Table Two, where you have a copy of the book you have just read. Here children will pass the book around the table. Each will take a turn showing a page of the story and talking about that page. If you have more than one copy of the story available, children can work in groups of two or three at this table, but all talk must be "Story Talk."

At the end, children each make up a question to ask the rest of the class about the story. Tell them that later you will be helping each of them write their question about the story. If they finish their Story Talk, they should retell it again, but start with a different person so that everyone gets to tell a different part than they told before. (The more you have practiced this strategy, the more effective this is.) Or, as they finish, they may go pick up a sentence strip and begin writing the question they will ask. Remind them that their questions must begin with one of these words: *who, what, where, when,* or *why.* For self-help, have question starter words posted for reference.

Story Talk in Action

Note: You would need to model this Story Talk strategy often with the class prior to this lesson. With practice, children become expert facilitators for each other in reinforcing manners, taking turns, clarifying points, and offering interpretations. The kindergartners in the following example have lots of practice in this strategy.)

Jenny: I'll start with the cover. It shows the two soldiers coming over the hill, but all these people in the little town are looking at them like, "What do you think you're doing?" It says the title is "Stone Soup." This word is *stone. (points to* stone, *then hands the book to Ivan)*

With modeling and practice, children become adept at retelling well-loved stories. Story Talk builds oral language skills, listening skills, sequencing, and comprehension. Children have the opportunity to create a question for their classmates based on the text.

Ivan: *(turns to the first story page and holds it up so everyone can see)* These guys see those other guys coming into their town and they think the other guys are gonna rob all their food and so they start figuring out how to hide their food. *(hands the book to Shaleen)*

Shaleen: *(points to one character hiding hams in a cupboard)* This really fat man, I think he was the butcher or something because he has that apron thing on, didn't want the soldier guys to see his meat . . .

Jenny: *(interrupts)* his ham

Shaleen: . . . his ham, so he's stuffing it behind his shelf thing, and I think it's going to get really yucky and stuff in there, and so then

Charina: *(takes book from Shaleen)* No, stop, now this page is my turn. So then the soldiers see all the people running all over and they know the people are hiding food so they know they have to make a plan or they won't get anything to eat.

Finally, explain that the third group will be working at Table Three, where you have clay on trays. These children will create a clay model of a scene or a character from the book. The sculptures will be on display for a day or two. Again, these children will need to generate a sentence or two about their model to write (or to have scripted) later.

Anyone who has worked at all in kindergarten will instinctively realize that some children assigned to illustrate will want to use the clay, and that some sculptors may want to retell the story, and that some of the storytellers may want to draw. It is important for children to know that, although they are initially responsible for completing their assigned task, the other materials will be left available and can be chosen as sponge activities. The literacy component (creating, writing, and reading a sentence) will only be done with their first task, unless they choose to do a sentence or question on their own at the other tables.

Differentiating for Readiness Levels to Support Literacy

No matter what their natural intelligence or preferred mode of learning, children must ultimately learn to read and write. Literacy must be an integral part of all that we do in kindergarten. In the above scenario, we have three distinct groups working on three distinct assignments. Each child in the groups mentioned earlier must be responsible for a sentence or a question about the story. Language Arts objectives include:

- Understanding sequence of events, characters, and setting in literature

- Using personal interpretation to respond to literature

- Using prewriting strategies (Do my words make sense? Do they sound right?)

- Using directionality of print in writing

- Dictating and/or writing with spelling approximations

- Turning oral language into print

It is at this point that the wide range of skill mastery and levels of readiness become most apparent. In the dialogue below, notice the different skills the teacher targets for each of the children after a reading of the folktale "Stone Soup." Also note that the teacher does not wait for each child to finish a task before she begins helping him or her with the sentence writing, which is the main objective of this lesson.

CHAD (Table 1: Illustrating a scene from the story and writing about it)

Chad is just beginning his illustration for the story when Ms. K checks in on his progress.

Ms. K: Chad, your drawing has a lot of faces in it. What would you like to say about your drawing?

Chad: These are all the people being happy when the soup was all done.

Ms. K: Great. Let's write just what you said now. Then you can go ahead and finish up your illustration. Do you want to write it on your drawing or on a story strip and then glue it on your drawing?

Chad: Write it here. (*points to space on drawing.*)

Ms. K: (*reads as she writes*) These are all _____ people being _____ when the soup was _____ done.

Chad and Ms. K: (*fingerpointing to the words*) These are all the people being happy when the soup was all done.

Ms. K knows that Chad recognizes a few sight words. When Chad gives a sentence with several sight words he knows, Ms. K purposely leaves out those words as she scripts his sentence. She knows this is a moderate challenge for Chad, but knows she has set him up for success in writing. When children use sight words in sentences that they create, the words become important to them.

Chad: (*pointing to blanks*): I know! *The* goes here, and *happy* goes here. (*points to correct spaces*) What's the last one again?

Ms. K: (*pointing to words as she reads*): when the soup was _____done.

Chad: All done.

When Ms. K reads aloud a sentence that has a blank in it, she says the word, "blank" as a verbal indication that something is missing. This technique can be used in whole-group writing lessons as well. You'll find that pairing this technique with pointing to each word with your finger (or with a pointer in whole group) helps you consistently reinforce left-to-right sweep and word-by-word awareness.

Ms. K: You've got it! I'll bet you can write the words for the blanks! If you need help, the words are on the word wall!

Chad: I only need help for *all*. I know *the* in my head! *T-h-e* is *the*, right?

Ms. K: Right! And the word *all* is somewhere else in your sentence, Chad. Let's point and read again.

Chad: (*pointing as he says words*): These are all the people . . . Hey, this word is *all*! (*points to* all)

Ms. K: (*gives Chad a smile and the thumbs-up sign as she is moving toward the next student.*)

Chad: And I know happy from our H-A-P-P-Y song!

Ms. K: (*throws Chad a big smile*)

■ **Brain Fact**

Brain researchers agree that immediate feedback is a powerful component for embedding learning (Jensen, 1998). Reward your children often with nonverbal warm-fuzzies like the thumbs-up sign, a smile, a wink, the A-OK sign. Whenever possible, include eye contact.

TAMARA (Table 2: Retelling the story in sequence with peers and generating a question)

Ms. K knows that Tamara has a strong command of letters and sounds and is ready for inventive spelling. She will use this opportunity to encourage Tamara to write words phonetically.

Ms. K: Tamara, let the others retell while you come over here with me and we'll write the words for your part.

Tamara: I told them about the page where the people were all afraid when they saw the guys coming, and they all hid their food, but that's not the part I really liked. I really liked it when the men fooled everybody and made them all bring all their carrots and potatoes and meat to put in the water 'cause it was only water really but when all the other people put all the stuff in at the end it was really soup and it was really good.

Ms. K: That's pretty much the whole story in a nutshell, isn't it? Can we make a question for your classmates?

Tamara: Oh, yeah, but I really do like how the farmer's bed was lumpy when he put his potatoes there.

Ms. K: You could ask a question about the farmer. I've got a story strip for you right here. Which word do you want to use to start your question?

Tamara: *Where.*

Ms. K: Okay, what will you ask with your *where*?

Tamara: Um… Where did the farmer hide his potatoes?

Ms. K: (*reads as she writes*) _____ did the _____ hide his potatoes_____ (*rereads with Tamara, pointing out that two blanks need whole words, and that one blank just needs a punctuation mark*). Use your letters and sounds to fill in the words. Do you know what mark goes at the end of a question?

Tamara: Course! A question mark! I might want to ask more questions, too.

Ms. K: Go right ahead, Miss Question Lady! (*Ms. K moves on.*)

Auditory learners love to hear themselves talk, and Tamara's rambling truly does show story comprehension. If Tamara herself had not narrowed her focus, Ms. K might have asked, "Which part made you laugh?" (Or "Which part did you like best?" or "Which character did the smartest thing?") Auditory learners will often need your help in narrowing their ideas.

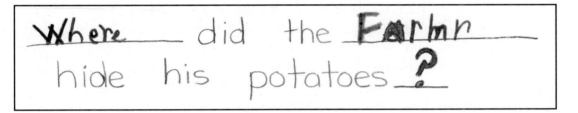

KYLE (Table 3: Making a clay model of a scene or character and writing a description)

Ms. K knows that Kyle is less verbal than most of his peers. She also knows that Kyle is struggling with letters and sounds, and therefore needs more cues and more support than many of his classmates. Yet she will not do all the scripting for Kyle, and will guide him to find success.

Ms. K: Kyle, it looks like a soup pot!

Kyle: Yeah, and it's big.

Ms. K: Sure is. I know you're not done, and you can go back to finishing the pot in a minute. Right now, we need to write your words. I have your sentence strip right here. What do you want to say about your sculpture?

Kyle: (*a man of few words!*) My pot's big.

Ms. K: You're right about that! Let's write this sentence: My pot is big. Here's what your sentence will look like. (*Ms. K writes* *and reads*) My ___ot is big. Now, Kyle, what do we need to turn *ot* into *pot*? (*Ms. K knows that Kyle is just beginning to master letters and sounds.*)

Kyle: I don't know.

Ms. K: Say *pot.* (*Ms. K emphasizes the /p/*)

Kyle: Pot.

Ms. K: Say "ot."

Kyle: ot.

Ms. K: What did we leave off?

Kyle: (*gives sound, not letter*) /p/

Ms. K: What letter says /p/?

Kyle: I don't know.

Ms. K: Go check the alphabet chart. /p/ is the letter *p*. On the alphabet chart, it's the pig sound. Find the pig and take a look at the letter. That's what you need to put in your blank.

Kyle: Oh, I know. That's like Peter's name!

Ms. K: You've got it Kyle! *Peter, pot,* and *pig* all start with *p*! Good detective work!

By naming the letter, giving the sound, and then directing Kyle to the alphabet chart, Ms. K encourages Kyle to visually find the letter. Like many children who are just developing an awareness of phonics, Kyle needs the picture clue, but he then makes an immediate connection to a friend's name. Ms. K celebrates the fact that Kyle has made the connection.

The three mini-lessons for Chad, Tamara, and Kyle take less than six minutes, total. The other children in the class are working, or have moved on to sponge activities or learning centers. After 20 minutes, Ms. K calls together the six children whose story strips have not yet been written.

Ms. K: I haven't done your story strips yet with you.

Ebony: I already took a strip and wrote my words. I put it in the basket.

Ms. K: Thanks, Ebony. I'll read it with you during center time. You may go clean up and get ready for gym.

Ms. K: For the rest of you, if you have a drawing or a model, put it on the display shelf with the others. We will do your story strips during center time or while we are washing for lunch. I can't wait to hear your ideas!

Once you are comfortable with teaching guided writing mini-lessons, you may find it efficient to write with two children at a time. While the child on your right is filling in words or letters or punctuation marks, the child sitting on your left is dictating to you. Over time, you will find student coaches who can help others by pointing out clues in the room or helping friends hear beginning sounds:

"When you're trying to hear a beginning sound, say the beginning sound three times before you say the whole word. Listen…/f/, /f/, /f/, foot. If your friend needs more help, tell them what the picture clue is on the alphabet chart."

By incorporating literacy into the follow-up art and discussion activities you already do with read-alouds, you can zero in on the specific skill each child needs while allowing each to find success. Ebony, in the scenario above, proudly announced that she had written her sentence strip with no help. Kyle was equally proud that he could make the connection between Peter's name and the /p/ sound. Both children were practicing new skills by building on the ones they already had while responding to the same piece of literature. The beauty of differentiated instruction is that children no longer compare themselves to others, but instead begin to take pride in personal growth.

Pride in personal growth (and the resulting confidence) is one important goal of differentiated instruction. The more you differentiate, the more growth you will see. However, instructional goals should drive the differentiation. No teacher can realistically differentiate all lessons for all children all the time.

Waiting until you can differentiate all lessons for all students flawlessly will guarantee that you will never differentiate any lesson for any student. On the other hand, differentiating your instruction by degrees, starting with an occasional, well-differentiated lesson, will keep you from being overwhelmed. You can evaluate, self-assess, modify, revamp, and find your own comfort level, just as you have from your first day of teaching. Start small, and make adjustments along the way.

Even experienced, skilled teachers who have been differentiating for some time do not attempt to differentiate every activity for every child every day. Set small but realistic goals for yourself. Plan to incorporate a differentiated lesson once a week or once during a theme. Move slowly away from the belief that all children must complete all activities, and you will soon catch the enthusiasm that children generate once they (and you) comfortably accept different children completing different activities.

Chapter 5

A Menu of Skill-Building Activities to Satisfy Every Learner's Appetite

Acomfortable way to start differentiating in kindergarten is to change, enhance, and expand the skill-building practice activities that you already are providing for your students. Current brain research tells us that practice does not necessarily "make perfect," according to the old axiom. Practice—with active engagement—makes permanent! As a skill or behavior is repeated, the neurons carrying the messages for that skill send increasingly stronger and more consistent messages to surrounding neurons. This strengthened connection between neurons allows for increasingly quicker recall (Pycha, 2000).

Indeed, children need practice, rehearsal, and repetition to embed learning. Yet we also know that active, hands-on skill practice that engages more than one area of the brain means more fun for children and enables more powerful learning than exclusively drill-and-skill-type practice because it engages more than one area of the brain. Completing more worksheets does *not* guarantee more learning. We know that children need to interact with learning materials and to build on what they already know. Worksheets typically offer one-size-fits-all drills with no meaningful connection or multisensory engagement, the key components for effortless learning (Bredekamp, Copple, & Neumann, 2000). Moreover, many kindergarten children haven't been "socialized" to make standardized academic responses posed by worksheets, making these an even less effective learning practice format for youngsters.

Academically focused curricula for preschool, kindergarten, and primary programs typically adopt a single pedagogical method dominated by workbooks and drill and practice of discrete skills. It is reasonable to assume that when a single teaching method is used for a diverse group of children, many of these children are likely to fail. The younger the children are, the greater the variety of teaching methods there should be, because the younger the children, the less likely they are to have been socialized into a standard way of responding to their social environment.

—Lilian Katz, *Another Look at What Should Young Children Be Learning* (1999)

As we confirmed in Chapter 2, kindergarten children joyfully explore all modalities of learning. Wise coach that you are, you understand that the more ways in which the skills are reinforced, the more neural pathways for retrieval are being built and the more likely it is that the skill will become permanent. You know that good teaching means letting children practice new skills in multiple ways.

Nearly every kindergarten teacher struggles daily to balance the rigorous academic expectations and standards of today's kindergarten with the play and exploration that build the readiness for those standards. Our instinct tells us to encourage creative play, hands-on fun, and active, physical learning. Our rank in the academic push-down now makes us accountable for skills that used to be deemed first-grade curriculum. Can we feel good about teaching those skills in a developmentally appropriate way? Can we engage and motivate learners of various modalities and intelligences without nightmarish planning and setup? Can we instruct in a whole-group setting without "aiming at the middle"? Can we design centers that are multilevel, allowing all learners to use the same materials?

Researchers studying the long-range effects of various teaching models suggest that overemphasizing academic work in the early childhood grades gives fairly good results on standardized tests in the short term, but may actually have the opposite effect over the long term (Marcon, 1995; Schweinhart and Weikart, 1997). Most young children are eager to make their teachers happy, and therefore accept that a worksheet is good for learning. But keep in mind the operative syllable in the word "*work*sheet."

Yes, yes, yes, and yes! Effective kindergarten teachers have been differentiating long before differentiation became a research-based best practice. Look carefully at the activities and centers that you use to reinforce skills. Most likely, you are already offering some variations in modalities (whether by design or by instinct). But does your skill-practice buffet table have something for everyone? Are you relying too often on worksheets for practice?

This chapter will give you ideas for whole-group activities and for learning centers that are academically sound and:

(a) encourage children to play, interact, and investigate,

(b) invite children to use all modalities: visual, auditory, and kinesthetic,

(c) give children at all levels a chance for success and growth, and

(d) offer children lots of kid-friendly practice to make skills permanent!

Fine-Motor Control: A *Learned* Skill

Although specific kindergarten standards and expectations vary slightly from state to state, all kindergarten children are expected to master certain academic skills and concepts before moving on to first grade. Kindergarten teachers know that important readiness skills, including essential pre-reading, prewriting, and pre-math skills *must* come first. Another crucial area of development is adeptness in fine-motor skills such as cutting, controlling a pencil, or using a paintbrush. Yet in the age of high standards (translate: teach more academics sooner), kindergarten teachers feel that they have no time to "waste" on teaching fine-motor skills in isolation. In a differentiated kindergarten classroom, the teacher provides children with countless opportunities to refine fine-motor skills while practicing literacy and math skills. Our challenge is to continually provide appropriate ways for children to strengthen fine-motor skills in the context of the ongoing curriculum.

Gross-motor skills like running, climbing, and jumping require lots of energy, which kindergarten children have in abundance. On the other hand, fine-motor skills require patience and eye-hand coordination, both of which can be in short supply in five- and six-year-olds.

The development of fine-motor skills is one of the two areas in which children will demonstrate the widest range of levels. (The other area is oral language.) Think of pencils, crayons, and scissors as musical instruments. Anyone learning to play the piano will spend weeks exercising the finger muscles by playing simple scales before they ever play a song. To ensure a successful performance, we methodically train the muscles that will perform.

That is true in music, in sports, *and in handwriting*. As wise teachers, we recognize the varying developmental levels of fine-motor precision among our students. We must give children frequent opportunities to increase finger strength and dexterity, and we offer a variety of ongoing activities to fortify weak muscles and to make strong muscles stronger. Children think they are playing; we know that we are teaching skills critical to their academic success while honoring their differences.

Writing Tools: One Size Fits Few!

By offering kindergarten children a variety of fun, hands-on fine-motor exercises, we encourage them to gain strength, control, and flexibility of the muscles in the hand.

Before we turn to center activities for fine-motor development, let's look at differentiating the writing tools you offer children. Consider this: Do all your kindergartners wear the same size sneaker or balance on one foot with the same ability? Of course not. The amount of growth, strength, and flexibility of the small muscles in your students' hands, and their experiences with writing tools, are also different from child to child. In fact, many of these children have not yet developed the dexterity and the elasticity of the inner palm that allows for a comfortable grip of *any* pencil!

How can we allow for the differing stages of fine-motor development? We can start by providing a pencil smorgasbord. Forget the notion that all your children must use identical writing tools. Offer a basket with a variety of writing tools for children to try out. You will find that after a few weeks of experimenting,

Teacher-Made Grips for Pencils

Even without manufactured grips, pencils can be customized easily and inexpensively. Buy a bag of practice golf balls, the plastic kind with holes, widely available at discount store, dollar stores, and sports stores. With a bit of effort, you can push a No. 2 pencil through the ball, creating a firm, round, grip that fits neatly into the young writer's palm.

The same effect can also be accomplished using plastic foam balls. The plastic foam does not last as long, but has the advantage of being available in varying sizes.

BE WARNED! Because most teacher-made grips are novel and toy-like, initially nearly all children will insist, "It fits my hand!" Have plenty available, and within a few days, the only children reaching for them will be the children for whom the ball grip is truly a good fit. The children who feel the grip is awkward or uncomfortable will soon abandon the novelty of it for a pencil with a better fit.

children will choose the pencil that feels most comfortable for their grip. The choices should include:

- traditional "fat" kindergarten pencils

- intermediate primary pencils

- standard No. 2 pencils

- any of the above with a variety of commercially available slide-on grips

- any of the above with teacher-made grips (see page 86)

Keep in mind that scissors, as well, are not one-size-fits-all tools. Like pencils, scissors come in a variety of styles, and children come with wide ranges of cutting experience. Again, offer a variety of plastic and metal, blunt ends and sharp ends. Let the children decide which pair best fits their own hands. Most manufacturers now make scissors that can be used by left- or right-handed children. If you do not have these scissors, you will initially need to patrol for appropriate handedness and let the left-handed children choose from scissors designed for them.

Learning Centers for Fine-Motor Skills...and Beyond

The following centers invite children to regularly exercise and strengthen fine-motor skills in engaging ways. They are also easy to assemble and inexpensive. All can be adapted as the year progresses to reinforce academic objectives, such as estimating or practicing sight words.

Pom-Pom Power: Build That Pincer Grip

Children enjoy opening and closing the tweezers to grasp, pick up, and place pom-poms in a bottle. In this center, children work the important muscles between the thumb and the rest of the fingers. In addition, they gain dexterity and flexibility of the palm.

Materials
- Several 12- or 16-ounce plastic juice bottles, both wide-necked and narrow-necked, without caps. (Thoroughly wash and put numbers on the bottles so each can be identified, to reuse for later math lessons, described below.)

- An assortment of tweezers in varying sizes, appetizer tongs, and salad tongs. (Try to provide one of each for each child who will be in the center at a time.)

- Five or six dozen colored pom-poms. (Pom-poms are best to use when introducing this center for fine-motor practice. You'll need two to three dozen pom-poms for each child working in the center.)

Procedure
Children fill one or more bottles with pom-poms, using any of the tools. They can then remove the pom-poms the same way.

Different Learners, Different Approaches
By providing small-necked bottles, wide-necked bottles, and a variety of tools, you will allow children to explore in ways that are comfortable to them. Children with strong fine-motor control will choose the smaller tweezers, smaller pom-poms, and smaller-necked bottles. Children will interact with this center in personal ways. Observing the children can offer clues about modalities and intelligences. Watch for children:

- layering the pom-poms in the bottles according to colors or sizes;

- making patterns with the colored pom-poms in the bottles;

- using tweezers in both hands to accomplish the job!

Add a sand timer to the center, and you'll find children challenging themselves and others to complete the task accurately at a faster speed.

Extensions
Reintroduce this center when you begin to teach the skill of estimation. Add a recording sheet. Have learners write their estimate of how many pom-poms (or buttons, macaroni, or other filler) they will use to fill a bottle. After they fill the bottle, they must empty it and count. They can make piles of tens to check the estimation. This is an excellent activity to reinforce what you have taught about grouping by tens to count quickly. By having a hundreds chart posted in this center, children who need a visual reference for counting by tens can do so independently.

Happy Hole Punching: Strengthen the Grip

Children sometimes come to school with well-developed fine-motor control, but very little strength in their grip. At first, centers that feature tools such as hole punches and large pushpins may be difficult or frustrating for these children since they require not just fine-motor dexterity, but also a robust grip. A firm, strong grip is necessary for future handwriting stamina.

Materials
- Several plastic food trays (the kind frozen dinners come in), or aluminum pie tins. With a hole punch, make a hole in the edge of each.

- Five to six inches of string for each tray

- Hole punches (enough for one per tray). Tie one hole punch to each tray.

- A variety of paper scraps for the children to punch: wallpaper, construction paper, sandpaper, aluminum foil, oaktag, junk mail.

Procedure
Children use a grip that is strong enough to punch holes in the paper. Show children how to hold the hole punch over the tray so that the punched-out paper dots fall directly into the tray. (Makes for easier cleanup!)

Different Learners, Different Approaches
Provide an array of materials and the children will naturally differentiate. Some will begin to make elaborate hole-punched patterns; some will find that they can fold the paper and create symmetry with the punched pattern; some will test their strength by punching multiple sheets. Others will try punching out letters or numbers. Children who need a lot of fine-motor practice can trace a pattern or a stencil to punch.

Extensions
Reintroduce the center with specific objectives to meet math standards. For sets and numbers, model the following task:

Punch one hole in a small strip of paper, two holes in the next, three holes in the next, and so on. Then write the corresponding number (or number word) on each strip and glue the strips in sequence.

When teaching symmetry, have children fold a paper in half and punch holes. They can connect the holes (similar to dot-to-dot drawing) or decorate the two sides identically to emphasize the symmetry.

Moving plastic eggs with salad tongs strengthens grip. Eggs can be labeled with letters or numbers to encourage spelling practice, ABC ordering, or number sequencing.

Transporting With Tongs: More Grip Practice

The colored plastic eggs that are so plentiful in spring can be used for several fine-motor, math, and phonics centers. For fine-motor practice, especially early in the year, children use salad tongs to pick the eggs from a basket and deposit them into empty egg cartons.

Materials
- Three or four dozen plastic eggs in a basket. For use later on, have several more dozen that can be labeled with letters, numbers, or sets.

- Several empty egg cartons. Collect many more to label with letters, number words, or sets.

- Salad tongs (one per child at the center). These come in a variety of fun styles and shapes.

Procedure
Children use salad tongs to pick eggs from the basket, one at a time, and deposit into the egg carton.

Different Learners, Different Approaches
The children themselves will show you variations. Some will sort eggs by color, and others will alternate the colors of the eggs to patterns. Add a sand timer, and watch the games begin as they challenge themselves and each other to fill an egg carton.

Extensions
Use a permanent marker to put a set of dots in the bottom of each egg cup, representing the numbers 1–12. Then label the eggs with a number 1–12 on the top half and the number words *one* to *twelve* on the lower half. Children now match eggs to the cup with the matching set in the egg carton.

Make another set of eggs with uppercase letters on one half and lowercase letters on the other half. Children match the letters. To keep it challenging, do not always put the uppercase on the same color egg as the lowercase form of that letter. Leave an alphabet strip at the center for self-checking and support. (This center activity does not require the salad tongs.)

Once children have learned a number of sight words, they can practice by spelling out words with the lettered eggs. Add a recording sheet for the list of words. Encourage children to write sentences using the sight words.

Printing With Pushpins: Eye-Hand Teaming

Using giant pushpins to create words pays dividends in big ways. It gives important fine-motor exercise, provides practice for making letters, and creates an end product (a dot-to-dot card of names or words) to reinforce reading and writing.

Materials
■ Giant-size bulletin board pushpins with colored grips that are the perfect size for little hands to grasp (sold in office supply stores).

■ Colored index cards with children's names, one name per card. Laminate for repeated use.

■ Blank index cards in a variety of colors to allow children to have a finished product.

■ Plastic foam meat trays or small squares of smooth carpet to provide a mat for sticking the pin into.

■ Stapler and staple remover

Be sure to model safe use of the pushpins! Explain that using the pins is a privilege (like so many other activities in the classroom), and that with every privilege comes a responsibility. Children who do not take responsibility, of course, lose the privilege. They may need to sit in the "Sugar Seat," get a bit sweeter, and have a second chance on another day!

Procedure
Children staple a blank index card to their laminated name card. Now they can "write" their name by inserting and removing the pushpin along the lines of each letter. By removing the staple when done, the children have a dot-to-dot card of their own name to keep and trace, while leaving their laminated card at the center for others to use. (Laminating makes the card reusable.) Because each child creates a "backup card," the plastic foam trays can be left for reuse at the center.

Different Learners, Different Approaches

Once they are comfortable with this center, some children will create a backup card by using a blank index card without their laminated model to "write" their name with the pushpins. Have a list at the center of all children's names.

Extensions

Later in the year, the large pushpins can be used to practice spelling sight words or to write word families. After the children create the words with the pins, they can connect the dots on the backup card and create their own stack of sight word cards.

Instead of writing their names on the cards, laminate simple outlined pictures from coloring books that relate to the themes you are doing. Children can staple construction paper to the laminated picture and trace the pictures with the pushpins. Once they have removed the construction paper from the laminated picture, they can color, decorate, and write a word or sentence. For example, during Underwater Week, this center could have blackline pictures of sea creatures.

We have explored some samples of fine-motor centers that are an important part of building academic skills. First let children simply explore, play, and interact with the materials to show you their different approaches. Later, consider using fine-motor centers as a more kid-friendly way to practice skills such as creating patterns with pom-poms, matching uppercase to lowercase letters using eggs and cartons, or reinforcing sight words by creating them with pushpins. The bonus: handwriting muscles are strengthening!

Allowing for Differences in Vision: Easy on the Eyes

It is important for kindergarten teachers to understand that children have varying levels of visual maturity when they enter our classrooms. Children must visually process two-dimensional print to read and write their names and to move on to all literacy activities. This means their eyes must work together and smoothly track across a page. Vision is developmental, and not all children are visually mature enough to effortlessly process black print on a white page in kindergarten. Before age eight, vision is strongly three-dimensional and peripheral (Hannaford, 1995). Early play experiences naturally encourage three-dimensional vision development, yet we often force an abrupt and often uncomfortable shift to two-dimensional print when the child enters kindergarten. We wouldn't assume that because a child is twelve months old, he has developed the muscles necessary to maintain balance or begin to take steps. Yet we persist in thinking that because a child is kindergarten age, visual maturity is a given, and he or she is physically ready to begin reading.

You can help children approach print with greater success with a few simple techniques in your classroom.

Configuring Words in Print

Wherever you post an important word, such as a common classroom tool, subject, or a child's name (on tables, at cubbies, on a word wall), cut it into the configuration that gives it a three-dimensional appearance:

Configuring print is a logical transition from three-dimensional to two-dimensional print. In addition to being less stressful for children's eyes, configuring helps reinforce the handwriting skill of distinguishing "tall letters, short letters, and below-the-line (long) letters!" Even though you are providing this visual cue especially for your visually young children, all children will benefit from seeing the out-line of the letter shapes defined. When the letters appear against a contrasting color, for instance blue letters set against a yellow background, the print appears more three-dimensional.

By having students' names printed in configuration and posted on a Name Board or Word Wall during the first week of school, you can immediately begin to make those powerful letter-sound connections for children through incidental instruction. Group together the names beginning with *A*, those beginning with *B*, and so on. (More ideas on building literacy skills with configured names are included later in the chapter.)

By configuring words that children will refer to repeatedly, you reinforce the correct size and shape of letters every time they see the word.

Should all words around the room be configured? No! (Imagine how visually chaotic a poster, calendar, or number chart would be if each word were outlined.) Configure only those words that the children will refer to most often in their own writing. Name Walls and Sight Word Walls are appropriate places for configuration in kindergarten.

Defining the Workspace

Define the visual field in which a child will work by providing a small but adequate surface for organizing letter shapes and other manipulatives: a felt mat, a tray, an egg carton lid, a carpet square, or another flat surface similar in size. This clearly delineates the work area and makes it easier for children to focus. The added bonus is that by choosing the right material to create a workspace, the drive-you-crazy noise of magnetic letters, dice, coins, dominoes, and teddy bear counters is greatly reduced. And reducing the noise level always reduces your stress level!

Think of the looking tube as exercise equipment for the eyes. As you regularly point out the configuration of names and sight words, as you frequently provide mats for a defined workspace, and as you occasionally ask children to use the looking tubes, you are providing lots of opportunities for all students to continue their visual growth from whatever stage they begin.

Providing Looking Tubes

Providing looking tubes, like configuring names and defining work areas, helps develop two-dimensional vision. Have a team of older students or parent volunteers cover toilet-tissue tubes with contact paper. Use a hole punch to put two holes opposite each other on the top, then thread with yarn, long shoestrings, or twine so the tool can be worn around the neck. Make an entire class set. Once covered, these are durable and can be used for several years before replacing. To keep twine or string from tangling when you store them, push the twine, string, or yarn into the center of the tube.

You may want to periodically bring out the looking tubes, and allow each child to wear one. For several minutes, let them freely explore with their "detective tools." Ask students to focus with one eye to find specific shapes, letters, patterns, or numbers in the room.

You might also lead children on a nature walk around your school and use the looking tubes to find a bird nest in a tree, the flag at the top of the pole, or a street sign on the corner. Take a tour inside your school and ask children to find with their tube the details they walk by every day, such as the fire extinguisher, the mobile hanging by the library, or a specific sight word on the title of the second-grade bulletin board.

With this simple tool in their hands, children become focused and motivated. You'll also learn about the different levels of visual maturity among your students. Children whose vision is still quite immature may not be able to decide which eye to use, or may hold the tube away from their face and try to look through it with both eyes. They will need lots of practice before they can close one eye and focus on a distant object. Watch for the children who cannot close one eye comfortably, but cover one eye with a hand. These children are also likely struggling to focus easily on two-dimensional print. Conversely, the child who confidently puts the looking tube to one eye, closes the other, and zeros in on an object is visually more ready for paper-and-pencil tasks.

Using Names for Early Literacy Activities

Many of the first phonemic awareness and phonics lessons we do in kindergarten involve the children's names. Effective teachers make frequent references to children's names, weaving them into each lesson: "Yes, our calendar says today is Friday. Look! *Friday* begins with the letter *f* and the /f/ sound just like *Francine*! That's the same as the frog picture on our alphabet chart." This simple comment, which takes less than 15 seconds, makes a powerful, multilevel connection for Francine and all her friends. Every child in the room, no matter how much exposure he or she has had with letters and sounds, can have a connection:

- For the child with poor phonemic awareness, you have isolated the sound.

- For the child with no concept of print, you have shown that a sound can be represented by a symbol.

- For the child who already understands concepts of print, you have connected a sound to a specific letter.

- For the child who is already reading, you have helped him or her read new words beginning with *f*.

You have also called attention to the sound and to the visual representation of the letter in the alphabet. By pointing out the frog picture, you have helped children connect with one more

For children coming to kindergarten unable to write even the first letter of their name, try a symbol or stamp system to keep track of papers and projects. Design a list of all student names, and beside each name, stamp a distinctive animal, symbol, or shape. Once a child recognizes his or her own stamp, he can proudly stamp his own paper. For children who can write their names but love the idea of stamping, allow them to first write their names and then make the stamp beside their names on their papers. As children become competent with name writing, remove the stamps. "Great! We're all writing our names well enough for us all to read our names! That means I can put away the stamps until we need them for one of our centers. Then you'll be able to use them all, not just the one that was yours for names!"

point of reference to help them remember the letter and sound *Ff*/f/. Similar comments, made every Friday, will have Francine and her friends recognizing this letter and phoneme long before you offer formal instruction for it. These opportunities for relevant, incidental instruction are especially effective for digraphs and irregular phonemes. "Look! It's /Th/-/Th/-Thursday again. There's that *t-h* sound just like it is in our sight word the and at the end of Kenneth's name!" Maybe little Bradley isn't ready for digraph instruction, or any phonics instruction for that matter, but by hearing these references over and over, his brain is building the neural connections he will need for the lightbulb to switch on.

Because we refer to names so often from day one, we want children to be able to quickly recognize and write their own names and the names of their classmates. However, any experienced kindergarten teacher will tell you that getting everyone on board with name writing can be daunting because:

a) as we have already learned, the fine-motor skills necessary to put pencil to paper for name writing range from nonexistent to mature,

b) the levels of visual maturity necessary for children to reproduce two-dimensional print range from weak to well developed, and

c) perfecting name writing and name recognition involves practice, practice, and more practice.

The following centers are designed to help children learn to recognize and read names (their own and those of their peers) while they continue to work their fine-motor muscles for handwriting. We'll address the role of vision in learning to write names and how we can help children who are still visually immature. Finally, we'll look at strategies that allow us to make every minute count by using name practice to teach phonemic awareness, phonics, and writing.

Practice, Practice, Practice: Differentiated Activities for Name Writing and Recognition

The following activities are designed to target specific modalities of learning, but they will appeal to all learners. You can feel confident knowing that each little brain will be building multiple pathways for retrieval of information. Remember, kindergarten children are exploring all modalities and all intelligences!

As soon as children recognize and write their own name, they become eager to master their friends' names.

Whole Group: Name Raps

Children create rap patterns to represent the sizes of letters in each name. For example, *Adam* would be "Adam, Adam, A-d-a-m: Tall-tall-short-short." Jenny would be "Jenny, Jenny, J-e-n-n-y: Tall-short-short-short-long." Make a large configured card for each name. As you hold up the card, you and the children "rap" the name.

> By recording the raps on tape, you can turn this activity into a center or a sponge activity. Just leave the cards and the tape at the listening center.

Whole Group: Names-ercise

Children and teacher decide on body movements that represent tall letters (arms reach straight up over head), short letters (arms bend at elbows, touching shoulders), and letters that go below the line (arms extend straight down by hips). *Patty* would be arms up, touch shoulders, arms up, arms up, arms down (tall, short, tall, tall, long).

Combine this with name raps to incorporate auditory and kinesthetic learning into a fun, energizing, team-building transition activity. When a student holds up the clearly printed name, visual learners have an anchor as well.

Center Activity: Configured Names

Materials
- Configured name cards, one for each child. Have a list of all class names available for self-checking.

- Writing paper or, to save paper, the configured names inside acetate sleeves. (An acetate sleeve is a sheet protector, usually used to preserve transparencies or protect pages in a document.)

- Dry-erase markers and erasers (for use on acetate sleeves)

Procedure

Children find and trace around the configured shape for their own name and for friends' names. They then write the names to fit within the shapes. Children can use dry-erase markers to trace and write. They can erase with a scrap of felt or a dry-board eraser.

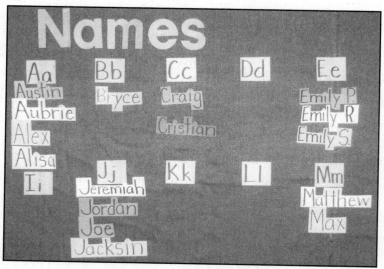

Configured names, with identifying photos on the back, help children see the shape of letters in their friends' names as well as their own.

Different Learners, Different Approaches

By providing the card and the list of classmate names, you have given all the tools necessary for every child to succeed. Differentiate one step further and put the child's picture on the back of his or her name card. For children already proficient at reading names, the pictures allow for self-checking. For children who are not yet recognizing all the names, you have added a visual to reinforce the connection of printed name to real-life friend.

Extensions

Extensions: leave writing paper at the center and challenge children to use their friends' names in sentences. The very confident learners will rise to the challenge and will surprise you when they begin to write names in lists: "Names that start like mine," or "Kids who sit at my table." You need to model an enrichment activity only once to get their wheels turning.

Center Activity: Name Grid

As the extension below shows, this is the activity that keeps on giving! By varying the Name Grid slightly, you can easily create motivating centers that will engage your learners in practicing phonics skills all year long.

Materials
■ Grid of all the first names of children. Prepare and laminate the grid on 9- by 12-inch oaktag. The size and number of boxes will depend on how many names you have. (Have an uneven number of names? Fill in extra boxes with your name, teacher assistant's name, or the gym, art, and music teachers' names.)

■ Grid of last names or initials (for later in the year)

■ Individual photos of each child that have been cut to match the size of the boxes. Each picture should have the child's first name, last name, and initials for self-checking. (The same pictures can be used for different grids.)

Procedure
Children match classmates' pictures to the names on grid. Then they turn the picture over to check that the name on the photo matches the name on the grid.

Extensions
Once children are successful in matching first names to pictures, try these options:

■ Make a grid using first *and* last names.

■ Create a grid with initials in each box.

■ Make a teacher and staff board using names and pictures of school personnel whom the children recognize.

■ Make and laminate multiple copies of any board, along with the pictures, to allow children to use them individually.

The Name Grid is an engaging activity for the beginning of the year, using names to jumpstart letter-sound association. Children learn to recognize classmates' names as they match pictures to names.

Center Activity: Build-a-Name

Materials
- Inch cube. (interlocking cubes also work.)

- Configured name cards. Use the name cards from the configured name center (see page 97).

Procedure
Children lay out cubes to make a three-dimensional replica of the configured name's shape to create the model of the name. Challenge children to find names that end up with exactly the same shape.

Center Activity: Clothespin Names

Materials
- Paint sticks (long, flat sticks for mixing paint). By drawing a smiley face on the left end of the paint stick, all children have a visual reminder of the starting point. "If your smiley face is right side up, you're at the correct beginning spot!"

- A zippered sandwich bag for each child

- Inside each bag, a card with the child's name on one side and picture on the other side

- Inside the bag, clothespins, each with one letter of the child's name on it

- A list of class names with identifying pictures for reference

- Paper on which to copy names created on paint stick

Procedure
Children find the bag with their picture and clip the letter clothespins onto the paint stick in the correct order to construct their names. (To help them with directionality, remind them to start at the smiley face.) Then they copy their names on a sheet of paper. They may also use the list of names at the center to write friends' names. Later in the year, encourage them to make a list of the names they have written or to use their name or a friend's in a sentence.

> ### ■ Tip!
> In spite of your careful modeling, clothespins at this center will eventually get all mixed up. Prepare ahead of time. Choose a symbol (green triangle, orange X, red star,) for each name, and label the back of each clothespin for that name with the symbol. Put the same symbol on the child's name/picture card. Now when the clothespins get all mixed up, sorting is easy.

The bonus is that opening and closing clothespins is an excellent way to build fine-motor strength!

Different Learners, Different Approaches

You can help children visually discriminate upper- and lowercase letters on the clothespins by writing the lowercases all in one color and uppercases in another color. Store the clothespin letters in a shallow box that can easily be carried from shelf to table.

Extensions

Clothespins with letters on them can be used for many centers throughout the year. For more time on task and less time spent sorting for the right letter, clothespins can be separated into cups, berry baskets, or clean, cut-off half-pint milk cartons. Put all upper- and lowercase *A*'s in one cup labeled "Aa," *B*'s in another cup labeled "Bb," and so on.

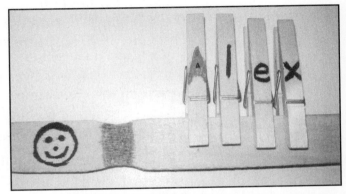

Strengthen fine-motor skills while reinforcing name recognition with clothespins on a paint stick.

All of the above tasks that practice name recognition and writing are designed so that a child at any skill level can be successful. Each child will bring to the task the skills already in place, and each will use the materials in the way that makes sense to him or her.

Differentiated Strategies for Moving Into Math: Through and Beyond September

By now, you are looking at your whole-group and center instruction and thinking, "Have I offered something for everyone?" "Am I keeping nearly everyone engaged nearly all the time?" (Don't be too hard on yourself. Remember, it would take a magic potion to engage all the children *all* of the time. We teach in real classrooms, not storybook rooms.) With time and practice, differentiation becomes a way of thinking, a model for planning, and a framework for instructing.

Working with sets and numbers, like name writing, is an ongoing, evolving process from day one in kindergarten. Let's take a look at some basic tools and activities that can lay the groundwork for successful differentiation in your math instruction.

A Look Inside a Differentiated Classroom:

It is early in the school year. The children and Ms. K are gathered on the rug. Today Jenna is sitting in the Champ's Chair because yesterday's "champ," Diego, drew Jenna's name from the pile of name cards. Jenna is today's Newsworthy Name.

Ms. K's objectives in the daily Newsworthy Name activity is to build phonemic awareness, draw attention to the phonetic qualities within each child's name, and build self-esteem and confidence as each child becomes the daily star of the show. She knows that the most interesting and meaningful word to most kindergarten children is their own name, followed by the names of people they care about (Mommy, Daddy, and friends' names). By using one name a day, Ms. K teaches early reading skills that are accessible to all children.

Together Ms. K and Jenna lead the class through all the name activities they have done with each Newsworthy Name. The class spells Jenna's name, raps Jenna's name, counts the letters, claps out the syllables, does a Names-ercise with the letters, and watches as Jenna cuts the letters on her name card apart and mixes them up in the pocket chart. Ms. K puts an uncut card of Jenna's configured name in the pocket chart and asks, "Jenna, do you want to reassemble your name, or do you want a friend to come up and do it?" Jenna chooses Audra, who bounces to the pocket chart and says, "I don't need to look at the card. I know how to do Jenna's name. She sits at my table."

Ms. K leads the group through a discussion of other names and words that begin with *J* and whether *j* is in the beginning, middle, or ending part of the alphabet. Everyone agrees that the alphabet picture of the j-j-jeep does indeed have the same beginning sound as *J-J-Jenna*.

Ms. K quickly reviews the rules and procedures for centers that the children have been working on this week and dismisses a few children at a time to check the Center Board to see which center they will complete today.

In a few minutes, Ms. K's classroom is quietly buzzing. Children, in groups of four and five, are working with their names and their friends' names.

Brendan, Rosa, and Bradley are working with Name Grids and Pictures. Brendan, a solid, adventurous learner, looks at the picture on the card and says, "That's Megan. I know her name starts with *M* and has a /g/ sound. That would be a g in the middle." Brendan lays Megan's picture on the word *Megan* and sees no need to check the back of the picture for verification. "Your turn," he announces as he pushes the Name Board toward Rosa.

Rosa, a competent learner, but not a risk taker, picks up a picture. Rosa says, "Oh, I know Robert. His name starts with my letter, *R*. Here's my name on the board. This other *R* must be Robert." Rosa turns the picture over, checks for Robert's name, and deposits the picture in the box on the grid.

Bradley is a hesitant, struggling learner, yet he approaches the name board with confidence. He picks up a picture and studies the face for a few seconds. He shrugs and turns the picture over to expose the name. He obviously neither recognizes the child nor can read the name, but Bradley begins moving the card from box to box on the grid until he proudly finds the letters that match the card he is holding. "Look, you guys, I found a match! It's him!" At this point, Bradley looks around the classroom, finds the classmate whose picture and name he has just matched, and points triumphantly to Mikey. Bradley, too, has found success, and has connected to his classmates while accessing important neural passageways.

Ms. K will keep the Name Grids and Pictures center available to children for five to six days, or until this center rotation is complete. She may then add it to the shelf of sponge activities as a free choice for an additional week or two. She knows the time invested in creating the center will pay off again later in the year when she brings it out again. With more skills and experience, children will then approach it differently. By adding a recording sheet to the center, she can ask children to write names, grouping them according to beginning sounds or number of claps (syllables), or to write sentences using the names once they have completed the grid.

As much as possible, integrate math instruction with literacy and thematic instruction. (Remember the graph, "We All Learned to Walk" from Chapter 4) Reasonably, many math problems have only one right answer: "How many more bunnies are there than ducks?" But a differentiated math lesson would include lots of open-ended questions or questions with more than one right answer. Train yourself to ask questions for which learners at all levels might have an answer:

Better Language for Learning	
TRADITIONAL QUESTIONS	**QUESTIONS THAT STIMULATE ALL LEARNERS**
Instead of:	*Ask:*
"How many more boys than girls are here today?"	"What do you notice about the number of boys and the number of girls that are here today?"
"What number comes next on the calendar?"	"What do we need to do to our calendar today?"
"How many more days until our field trip?"	"How could we figure out how long it will be until our field trip?"
"What is 3 plus 2?"	"How many different ways could we make a set of 5?"

Building Math Skills for All Learners

Many children can count by rote when they come to kindergarten, but few come able to correctly form numerals or write numbers in sequence. Like name writing, this skill involves more than cognitive understanding. A child needs fine-motor and visual maturity to master number writing.

The whole-group and center activities that follow give children practice in matching sets to numbers, recognizing numbers, and writing numbers, all critical prerequisites for math instruction. Most employ more than one modality of learning and several intelligences, and they therefore appeal to a wide variety of learners and also give more children opportunities to feel successful. Brain research continues to remind us that using multiple strategies for learning, and varying the ways in which children interact with materials, greatly increases the chances for recall and transfer of knowledge.

Whole Group: Number Rhymes

Brain research validates the commonly held notion that talking anchors learning, and that rhythmic language is a powerful memory maker for embedding learning. Kindergarten children love to sing, rap, and play with language. Use that natural instinct to enhance their learning.

As you instruct children in sets and numbers, teach children the number rhymes that follow. For your visual learners, be sure to hold up the corresponding number so they can see it as they say it. Auditory learners will especially enjoy changing the beat into a peppy cheer, a monster voice, or a sing-songy rhyme. Your kinesthetic learners will love large, exaggerated "air-writing" of the numbers as you say the rhymes.

Write the rhymes on chart paper and laminate them. Use the charts for shared reading, choral speaking, and sight-word identification. You'll be teaching reading *while* you're teaching handwriting and math.

Whole Group: Air Writing Numbers

As you teach the number rhymes, children write the numbers in the air. Let them experiment with gestures. Air-write using a fist, two fingers, a pointer finger, a toe, an elbow.

Whole Group: Numbers Outside

On the playground, provide sidewalk chalk for the children to freely practice saying the number rhymes while making the numbers. Draw a large number on the pavement. Model walking the number while repeating the rhyme.

Take buckets of water and paintbrushes outside. As children say the number rhymes, they paint the numbers on the school wall. You can

Memory Making Number Rhymes

0
Round and round
Makes a zero.
A circle round
Is a badge for a hero.

5
A bee flies out,
Dives down from the hive.
Backs around the bush,
And makes a five!

1
A straight line down,
Then you're done.
That's the way
We make a one!

6
Down to
A hoop,
A six
Makes a loop!

2
Half a heart,
But you're not through,
A line to the right,
Now that's a two!

7
From left to right,
And down from heaven,
That's the way
We make a seven!

3
Around a tree,
Around a tree,
That's the way
We make a three.

8
Eight starts like S,
But don't you wait,
Go right back up
And close the gate!

4
Come down, turn right,
Come down once more.
That's the way
We make a four!

9
Make a balloon,
Slide down the line,
That's the way
We make a nine!

also let them use spray bottles to write the numbers, but remember that squeezing the trigger of a spray bottle requires strong grip and will tire little hands quickly.

Center Activity: Color-Coded Number Tracing

Materials
- A set of number cards that show correct number formation of each number by strokes highlighted in color: green for the first stroke, blue for the second, and red for the third. A dot and an arrow further illustrate where to start and the direction in which to go. The number 1 will be all in green: 2 will show the initial upward, then downward curve in green, but the second stroke that forms the bottom would be blue, and so forth. Put the corresponding number of dots in the upper left of each card, as well as the written number word. Now the cards are reinforcing sets and numbers for your budding math munchkins, and they also add a literacy component for the readers in your class.

- Acetate sleeves (page protectors)

- Dry-erase markers and erasers (Old socks work well for erasing acetate sleeves.)

Cards that show correct number formation can be purchased commercially. If you have a set, simply use a permanent marker to add dots or other symbols to show the visual representation of the set for that number. In addition, write the corresponding number word on the card. Now all learners have a point of reference: they can see the number, count the set, and mentally connect the word. You've accessed multiple neural pathways of retrieval, each of which may be important to a different learner.

Procedure
Children insert a number card into an acetate sleeve and trace it with a finger or with dry-erase markers that will wipe away with a white-board eraser or an old sock. The additional space on the acetate sleeve can be used to practice the number without tracing, to write the number word, or to draw a set of that number of objects.

To increase retention and delight your auditory learners, encourage children to quietly recite each number chant as they work.

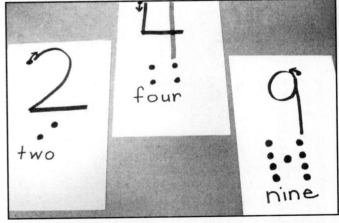

Children practice correct number formation by tracing cards in an acetate sleeve. Visual clues reinforce sets and number words. While tracing numbers in acetate sleeves, children get reams of practice without using reams of paper. This quick-erase activity has the feel of the ever-popular magic slate toys.

Center Activity: Clay Numbers

Working with clay strengthens fine-motor muscles and, engages kinesthetic-tactile learners, and it's fun!

Materials
- Use the laminated cards prepared for the above center, or prepare an additional set.

- Clay or play dough. (See page 67 for a scented play dough recipe and tips on keeping this center germ-free.)

Procedure
Children make "snakes" of clay and mold the clay into the correct numeral, either right on the card or beside the card. Once again, they can make small clay balls to represent the set.

Of course, encourage out-loud recitation of the number rhymes. As a child completes his number, he traces and recites.

Center Activity: Matching Magnetic Numbers

Magnetic numbers can be used for sequencing on a metal cookie sheet, and they are also effective manipulatives for practicing number recognition and writing.

Materials
- Magnetic numerals, 0–9.

- Number cards. Make these by tracing around the magnetic numerals. Laminate for durability. Put dots in the corner to reinforce the set-to-number relationship, and write the number word to reinforce word recognition.

- Acetate sheets

- Dry-erase markers and erasers

Procedure
Children slide the number tracings into an acetate sheet and match the magnetic letters to the outlines. Since the acetate sheets will wipe off after using a dry-erase marker, suggest that children also write the number, the number word, or both on the card or

---

■ **Tip!**

Choose your magnetic numerals carefully. Look especially at how the numerals 1 and 4 are made. Most kindergarten math programs teach children to make the number four with a straight, open top (4) rather than with an angular top (4), and to make the number one with a single stroke, no slash (1) Children need to recognize both forms as numbers, but they need to be instructed to write the numeral according to your math program. You can acknowledge the differences and confirm for children the correct model by saying, "Oh, yes, that's the computer (or typewriter) way to make a 4. Our kindergarten 4 looks like this...."

acetate sheet beside each magnetic tracing. Some children will trace the tracings. All will be making set, number, and number-writing connections.

Whole-Group or Center Activity: Before and After

This skill sheet for practicing number writing also encourages higher-order thinking. While children rehearse correct number formation, they practice number order.

Materials
■ A die. Make a die with dots and a die with numbers available.

■ A felt mat on which to roll the die

■ A number line or chart (for self-checking or for support)

■ The recording sheet (page 111)

Procedure
Children choose a die to roll. They identify and write the number they have rolled on a sheet of paper. Then they identify and write the number before and the number after this number.

Different Learners, Different Approaches
This multilevel activity has something to teach all children. Children who can visually recognize a set and connect it to a number will choose the die with dots and convert the dots to a number on their sheet. Children still unsure of set-to-number relationship can choose the die with numbers.

Create a number line like the following for children to use when doing the activity. In one place, children can see the set, the number, and the number word. The number line is there also to help identify numbers. (Some children will need to start at zero

> Whenever possible, avoid calling practice sheets "worksheets." Vocabulary is powerful, and children will have less negative associations to words such as *skill sheet*, *practice sheet*, or *activity sheet*. You might even use the term *WowSheet*. Let them know this is their chance to "wow" you with their skill.

A number line with sets, numbers, and number words is a useful tool for all learners.

each time and count to "their" number in order to name it.) For enrichment, challenge your students to use number words instead of numerals.

Extensions

Provide for your readers dice labeled with number words instead of dots or numerals. Later in the year, use dice with numbers beyond six. You can buy these or make them out of one-inch wooden cubes available through teacher supply houses. When working with two-digit numbers, have children roll two dice to create a number.

Mnemonic Math

The teen numbers, especially 11, 12, and 13, are typically difficult for many kindergarten children. The words *eleven*, *twelve*, and *thirteen* are not easily connected by children to the sets. Any of the above activities could be extended to recognizing and writing the teen numbers.

Get creative! Use these or similar silly memory-jogging rhymes:

A one beside a one,
Floating down from heaven
That's ten plus one,
And that makes eleven!

A one beside a two
Sitting on a shelve,
That's ten plus two,
And that makes twelve!

A one beside a three
Showing up on our screen,
That's ten plus three,
And that makes thirteen!

Before and After My Number

Name_____

Instructions to read to students:

1. Roll a die and write the number in the "My Number" column.

2. Write the number that comes before it in the "Before" column.

3. Write the number that comes after it in the "After" column.

4. Try another! If you roll the same number again, keep rolling.

Before	My Number	After

A Look Inside a Differentiated Classroom

Ms. K and her class have been exploring the math concept of "equal."

Now Ms. K asks Reggie to come up, close his eyes, and choose a number card. "Don't show it to anyone," she whispers. Reggie looks at the number he has chosen, and silently points to and counts the dots on the number card. Ms. K knows that Reggie still needs the sets to help recognize numbers. Reggie instinctively knows this too, but instead of saying, "I don't know this number," he immediately counts the dots. He's learned a self-help strategy!

"I counted the dots just to be sure, but I know the number," Reggie boasts.

"Yes, we know that Reggie is good at counting, don't we, boys and girls?" The children all nod as Reggie beams. With a simple sentence, Ms. K affirms Reggie's skill with numbers and subtly validates this strength to the rest of the class.

"Now, Reggie, give me your number card. Name as many friends to stand at the back of the rug as you need to equal that number. Remember, don't tell us your number. Boys and girls, the rest of us will figure out the number in our heads. Duck lips, so no one says it out loud!" "Duck lips" is the visual and kinesthetic clue some children need to remember not to shout out an answer: The children purse their lips together to form a duck beak. Some pinch their lips together with their fingers.

Reggie appears to be deep in thought. "Um, Danny, go. And Warren, and Matt, and, um... Harry, and, " Reggie looks down at his hands as he counts on his fingers. "Okay, I need one more. Dickie, go stand at the back."

"Does the number of children equal the number on your card?" asks Ms. K

"Yep."

"Okay, math detectives. Raise your hand if you can name a number that is more than the number you think Reggie chose," Ms. K challenges. She knows that some children need the challenge of finding numbers of greater or and lesser value, while others need the exposure to the vocabulary and the concept.

After accepting a few correct answers, Ms. K asks for numbers less than Reggie's number. Finally, she asks what all children have been dying to answer.

"On the count of three, everyone who thinks they know Reggie's number needs to put up that many fingers, and say the number. One . . . two . . . three . . . "

"Five!" Little hands with five fingers outstretched wave in front of Ms. K. The five boys at the back of the rug join in also. By encouraging answers in unison, Ms. K has allowed the confident children to show that they know, the shy children to answer without being singled out, the unsure child to hear the correct answer, and the child with the incorrect answer a chance to hear the right answer without being embarrassed.

"Yes, f-i-v-e- five! Are we right, Reggie?" Reggie nods. "Okay, take a deep breath. Raise your hand if you can put an equal number of children standing at the front of the rug. Boys at the back, stand straight and tall and still. We may need to count you again."

Ms. K goes through a similar procedure with letting Rayna and Ashley be the math leaders.

To follow this activity, Ms. K reads *The Doorbell Rang* by Pat Hutchins. She reads the complete story first, then rereads, stopping each time the doorbell rings.

"How do we solve the problem and make sure everyone now gets an equal number of cookies?" she asks.

Each time another child in the story arrives, one of Ms. K's students comes to the flannel board and moves around the felt cookies to divide them equally among the felt children: two, three, four, six, and twelve. Ms. K urges each child to "think out loud, and tell us how you're solving the problem." She makes certain to validate each child's approach.

Ms. K knows the children need meaningful, personal experiences like these to learn math concepts. She purposely structures math lessons that incorporate movement and music, allowing children to learn while actively engaging with their peers.

Differentiating Using Kindergarten Class Books

A class book is a powerful instructional tool and an effective cumulative review of a theme. Each child is the author and illustrator of one page. Once the book is assembled, it can be added to the class library for a few days and then sent to homes on a rotating basis. Include a page at the beginning that allows families to sign and write comments.

Children get a chance to be expressive and creative, and to revisit content of a theme or react to a story. As children are creating, teachers can do individual (differentiated) mini-lessons for writing (as we saw Ms. K do in Chapter 4).

The finished product is a work of the classroom team, and it becomes one more way of fostering an attitude of cooperation and community.

Class books serve also as an effective conduit for home-school literacy connections. Parents can stay informed about themes and curriculum when children take class books home and share with their families.

Allowing All Children to Be Successful Authors in a Class Book

Several formats provide structure for class books. Choose a format tailored to your specific instructional objectives based upon the theme you are summarizing, the specific skill you are teaching, or the literary response you are inviting. The simplest, most effective formats for a class book are pages with preprinted text, sentences from predictable charts, and children's paintings and drawings as story starters.

Class Book format: Pages printed with preprinted text.

Each child receives a page with a preprinted text prompt and a part to fill in. For example: "If I had a farm, I would raise _____." The text might reflect a current theme, such as farms, in response to a book that was read. Children complete the sentence and illustrate their words. Give students options for completing their page to challenge students who are ready to take on a more involved writing task, to encourage

> Children can write and illustrate their class book pages as whole-group independent work or in centers. For most students, you will need to be available to prompt or to scribe, but children can do their illustrations while waiting for you. As they become more confident in inventive spelling, you will be less involved in the actual writing.

students who may be reluctant to take a risk, and to assist students who need extra support. You might tell the children: "Use your kindergarten spelling to write an animal name. If you'd like, write an additional word, phrase, or sentence about your picture. . . ." (These are the adventurous learners!) "Or, you can go to the list of theme words and pictures on the wall for this unit to help you write the name of an animal. . . ." (These learners are competent, but lack confidence!) "Or, decide on an animal and write the beginning letter that you hear, and the ending letter, and any other letters that you hear in the middle of the word." (These learners need more support.)

When scripting for these children, acknowledge what they can do. "You want to write horse, Mary? You heard and wrote the *h*! Good! I am going to write '-o-r- (blank) -e.' Let's say the word and decide what letter needs to go in the blank." The child then writes the appropriate letter. This student may need direction to a picture alphabet posted in the room. "You need to find the s-s-snake picture to help you with the letter."

The family comment page at the front of the book might look like this:

<u>*The Morgans*</u>   If we had a farm, we'd like to raise <u> *sheep* </u>.
(family's name)   (family's response)

Class Book Format: Sentences From a Predictable Chart

Creating a predictable chart is a logical follow-up activity after reading a predictable big book. With repetitive language, predictable text builds fluency and allows beginning readers to focus on the meaning and sound of the words instead of exclusively on decoding them. Children who are creating (and following) predictable text are learning concepts of print and building awareness of syntax and context, as well as reading and writing content.

To create a predictable chart, introduce the first line of the predictable text, adding your own ending. Ask each child to contribute a new sentence, following your model. Write their sentence as they dictate. Since kindergarten children frequently become restless after four or five of their peers have contributed sentences, add only a few sentences at a time, making this an ongoing chart. It may take three or four days for everyone to add a sentence. Begin each day by reading together the sentences already written. Let a student "Reader Leader" use a pointer to direct the choral reading.

Predictable charts can also be an opportunity to "share the pen." After writing the predictable text, children can be invited to come and complete the sentence with their word(s) using kindergarten (inventive) spelling.

Many of the predictable charts that you and your class create can become useful class books. A predictable chart created during a unit on careers and community helpers may begin like this:

I will be a teacher. (Ms. K)

I will be a garbage man. (Kyle)

I will be a ballet dancer. (Sharon)

I will be a teacher. (Darby)

I will be a truck driver. (Hannah)

I will be a circus clown. (Johann)

After the chart has been used for shared reading and whole-group instruction, cut apart and clip together the words of each child's sentence, or put each cut-apart sentence in a baggie or an envelope. Let the children arrange and glue the words on a piece of drawing paper and then illustrate. (The paper must be large enough to accommodate the cut-apart sentences. Or, type the sentences in large font, print, and cut apart.) The child's page then becomes one page of the class book. This strategy allows nonreaders to use beginning sound clues and sight-word clues to "write" their sentences. Competent writers, however, can be encouraged to add to their sentences once they are sequenced and glued, or to copy them as they are.

You might use the following prompt for the family comment page at the beginning of the careers class book:

Juan's family
(family name)

We think being a ___*diplomat*___ would be a great career because . . .
a diplomat travels the world and helps countries solve problems like war and food shortages.
(family's response)

Format for Class Book: Children's Paintings and Drawings as "Story Starters"

When using scripted pages or predictable chart sentences, the writing comes before the illustration and helps shape the illustration. At other times, the child's drawing should be the inspiration for the words. In these cases, it is appropriate for the teacher (or aid, volunteer, or older student helper) to script since children usually have a lot to say about their drawings! Whenever possible while scripting, leave blank spaces for words, sight words, or beginning or ending letters for the student to complete. Some students will be able to write a great deal on their own; others will need considerable help. The strategy that Ms. K used for helping children write about "Stone Soup" (in Chapter 2) will help students at all levels express their own ideas.

Kindergarten children ramble when describing their own drawings. This is a powerful opportunity for instructive modeling. Shanique may say, "That's my cat and she isn't really very big and I got her from my uncle, but in my picture she's up in the tree because Joey's dog is mean and chases her and one time that dog scared her really, really bad, and this is me over here in my red jacket." The teacher can say, "May I rearrange your words a little bit to fit on the picture?" Shanique nods, and the teacher says, "Let's write, 'My little cat got chased up the tree. I had on my red jacket.' " The teacher then writes as much or as little as Shanique needs, and Shanique does the rest.

Notice that the young authors of these pages are obviously at different stages in their literacy journey. Yet each child was set up to succeed because the teacher gave options and provided tools for completing the class book page.

Peter welcomed the challenge to work independently. He used inventive spelling to give a detail about the horse.

Carrie checked the list of farm animals that the class had generated. She wrote the word *sheep* twice and appears to have written "Baaa....."

Kyle dictated words that were scripted by the teacher, who left blanks for Kyle to fill in. He was able to hear and write the *b* in *black*, and the *c* in *cow*.

Each contributed to the class book, each practiced writing skills, each received on-the-spot instruction to suit their own needs, and each felt successful.

Expanding the Choices: Differentiated Materials and Tools

We consciously try to use differentiated strategies, lessons, and processes. Honoring each child as a unique learner is a goal that we must set for each year, for each day, and for each lesson. Much of what you already do in your classroom, as well as many of the materials you already use, encourages differentiated learning.

It's not about how smart they are; it's about how they are smart.
—HOWARD GARDNER

Take stock of the instructional tools you use regularly. Make certain there are activities that will attract every kind of learner. For an overview of materials that encourage learning styles, refer to the chart "Strategies to Engage All Learners" on page 25 in Chapter 2.

Tips and Tricks for Managing the Differentiated Classroom

Giving all learners a chance to succeed means providing choices within the classroom environment that may give a "leg up" to developmentally young or struggling learners, as well as reinforce learners of varying modalities. Making some simple accommodations in the physical setup of your classroom and lessons will ensure that each child can perform optimally, and often makes classroom management easier for you.

As any experienced teacher can tell you, not all discipline and management strategies are effective with all children. An effective teacher takes time and effort early in the school year to observe behaviors and reactions, and molds the classroom so that all students become as self-directed and self-managed as possible. By incorporating a wide variety of management tools and strategies, you can ensure that you are allowing for the many personalities and learning styles in your kindergarten. The following specific techniques will cover a wide range of learning and behavioral issues.

Whisper Phones

These simple tools, shaped like a telephone receiver, allow a child to speak into one end and to immediately hear his or her own voice from the other end. (You can find commercially manufactured whisper phones, or you can make them from PVC pipe, as described at right.)

Use PVC pipe to inexpensively make a class set of whisper phones. Buy an eight-foot piece of one-inch PVC pipe and two 1-inch PVC elbows for each phone from a local hardware store. Cut the length into 4-inch segments. Most stores, for a few pennies a cut, will do it for you. Position a PVC elbow at either end, and you have a "phone," just the right size for little hands. You can also, for a few more dollars, purchase PVC pipe already in a "C" shape that needs no additional pieces.

This tool is especially valuable for the auditory learner because it immediately reinforces the sound being focused upon. In the kindergarten classroom, it is effective in reinforcing letters and sounds. We call it the whisper phone, since to do anything other than whisper actually hurts your ears! Whisper phones are a powerful aid in helping children use their knowledge of phonics to do inventive spelling. When a child says a syllable very slowly into the whisper phone, he or she can more easily distinguish the individual phonemes.

Model the use and purpose of the whisper phone, and leave a basket of them out for any child to use when reading to himself or when sounding out words for writing. By encouraging children to use a whisper phone whenever they are reading or counting "to themselves," you help them naturally process their internal thoughts with their outer voice, and you lower the volume in your classroom.

A whisper phone helps with counting, reading and with inventive spelling.

Fidgets

Fidgets are any noiseless squeeze toy that a child can hold while focusing attention on you or listening to classmates. They can be spongy balls, beanbags, small stuffed animals, balls of clay, or corn-starch-filled balloons. Children are allowed to hold them while seated on the rug, as long as the fidgeting does not interfere with their listening or with their neighbors' listening.

Of course, expectations must be clear for the appropriate use of a fidget, or chaos will prevail. Like all other privileges in your classroom, a fidget is taken away from any child who chooses to use it in an inappropriate way. "With every privilege comes a responsibility, boys and girls. Using a fidget is a privilege!"

Fidgets are not only effective for children. Many adults, when listening to a speaker, find they can better focus on the words if their hands are engaged: doodling, knitting, kneading.

For many children, especially those with emotional stressors or nervous habits, the act of unconsciously kneading or stroking is calming and helps focus their attention. You know the child: if you don't give her something to do with her hands, she will find something, and it could involve someone else's hair, her sneaker strap, or an unraveling thread. None of those "fidgets" have pleasant outcomes!

The Daily Dose of Attention: Teacher, Look at Me!

Kindergarten children are hardwired to want the attention of other children and adults. Affirmation and validation are daily requirements for these youngsters, no matter how immature or academically astute. Below you'll find some quick and simple ways to give all children the attention they crave—even the ones who do not blatantly demand your attention.

As you consider the activities below, keep in mind that although all children at this age have a need for attention, not all will demand it. Know that all children, including the less verbal, less insistent, and less clamorous also have a basic daily minimal requirement for adult interaction. While responding to the needs of the children who are calling your name, tugging on your shirt, and grabbing for your hand, be sure also to acknowledge the cooperative, well-mannered, respectful children. They may not be as obvious about it, but they too have little hearts that jump for joy when they notice that they are noticed!

Eyeball to Eyeball.

Make a conscious effort to acknowledge each child's arrival every day by looking him or her in the eye and greeting him or her by name. "Good morning, Jason." "Nice haircut, Terry." "Let me read your T-shirt, Tamara." (Note: In some cultures, it is considered offensive to look someone in the eye, or to maintain eye contact. Know your student population. In such a case, an appropriate touch on the shoulder or arm as you deliver the greeting will accomplish a similar reaction.)

The Can-Do Cards.

You're not the only caring adult in the building. Children gain self-confidence and can reinforce learning by interacting with other teachers and staff. Lay a little groundwork ahead of time, and you can enlist the aid of other nurturers to give your children the attention they need.

Laminate a set of small cards, each with an appropriate kindergarten task:

Watch me tie my shoe!

Can I read this list of words to you?

Ask me my phone number.

Listen to me spell my name.

May I count by 10's to 100 for you?

I know these sight words!

Vary the levels of the tasks, so that there are reasonable ones for every child.

Arrange ahead of time for your children to occasionally get special attention from other cooperative adults in your building. Ask who would be willing to have your children visit them during morning time, dismissal time, recess time, or lunchtime. When your kindergarten child shows up with the card, the other adult need only take the one-minute or less necessary to let the child show mastery of the task on the card.

> ### ■ Brain Fact
>
> Research confirms that when you look someone in the eye in a sincere, caring manner, and at the same time say their name in a non-threatening way with an appropriate voice, the brain responds positively. From an early age, children learn to connect caring eye contact with safety and sincere concern (Farroni, Csibra, Simion, and Johnson, 2002). Meeting a person's non-threatening gaze lights up the areas of the brain associated with rewards (O'Meara, 2002). This quick morning greeting can help your distressed students open learning channels.

Children are proud to show off their newly learned skills to special-area teachers, the school secretary, the nurse, the principal, the custodian, and others. Let these people know that if a child appears at an inconvenient time, it is perfectly all right to tell the child to come back later or to put a sticky note on the card indicating a better time. Even though we want to let children interact with caring adults, children do need to learn that the world does not always stop turning when they would like attention.

Through careful, conscious design of our centers, our activities, and our daily interaction with children, we set a rich table of learning from which all children can feast. The specific ideas and strategies from Chapter 5 will give you a solid base upon which you can build to differentiate your classroom and your instruction. Don't overwhelm yourself by attempting too many innovations too quickly. Acknowledge the areas in which you are already differentiating for students, and recognize the areas where you could make your good teaching even better. For every moment you spend preparing to differentiate in your classroom, you will be rewarded by the hugs, comments, and learning success of the little folks who say to you, "I really like kindergarten!"

Final Thoughts

The goal of a differentiated kindergarten classroom is to embrace all children as successful learners. This means accepting them where they are when they enter, and offering them instruction and activities in many different ways that allow learning at many different levels. No one has found a neat formula for differentiating in every circumstance. In each situation, you must consider the child's readiness and background of experience, as well as his or her interests, strengths, and needs. The degree to which you differentiate your classroom will depend greatly upon *your* teaching style, preferences, and experience.

Early in Chapter 1, we considered the questions that every child-centered teacher asks himself or herself frequently. Let's revisit those questions, this time as a reproducible page that you can keep at your fingertips for reference. Use the questions as guideposts for your efforts to make your room the best kindergarten room it can be.

See your classroom not just as the place where learning can happen, but as the medium for learning. We know now that a

Does My Classroom Offer All Children an Even Playing Field?

■ Do I have high expectations for all children?

■ Do I model respect for all children's work?

■ Do I consciously integrate physical movement, music, and art into lessons?

■ Do I have free-play centers for building, drawing, reading, imagining, exploring?

■ Do children have choices in materials, centers, and assignments?

■ Do I use time flexibly?

■ Do I incorporate whole-group instruction, small-group instruction, and one-on-one instruction?

■ Is the composition of my small groups flexible and ever changing?

■ Do I use ongoing, authentic assessment and "kid-watching" to adjust and evaluate teaching as well as learning?

■ Do I assess children according to their individual growth?

■ Are children relaxed, eager, and actively engaged?

■ Are there times in my room when children are working on a lot of different activities?

■ Do I vary my teaching style, ask open-ended questions, and initiate discussions?

■ Are children involved in classroom problem solving?

child-centered classroom, a classroom that is dynamic and ever changing to reflect the needs of the children, is the best environment for a child to learn to love learning. In the 1960s Maria Montessori laid some important groundwork for teachers seeking to teach *children*, not curriculum. Today's kindergarten teacher juggles standards, scheduling, and paperwork, but always puts the child at the center of his or her energy.

We began the Introduction of this book by quoting from a textbook for teacher training dated 1916. Many changes in our world have impacted education since 1916: family structure, societal expectations and mores, experiences before age five, and technology. Yet much of what was viewed as good teaching in 1916 is still considered good teaching:

"Boys and girls must grow into the fullness of life themselves. Growth is not mechanical. We can only supply the necessary environment. When we try to teach all children by the same method, the result narrows and deadens. The teacher's aim is to awaken in the child what the lesson has to say to him" (Beecher & Faxon, pages 19–20).

Good teaching is, was, and always will be about how the children learn. And that means honoring differences among children, looking for strengths in each child, and paving the road for each child to find "what the lesson has to say to him." Differentiated kindergarten is about children, not about teachers. The teacher's role is to invite learning through solid, research-based strategies offered in a nurturing, supportive environment.

Professional References

Bafile, C. (2006). Different strokes for little folks: An interview with Carol Ann Tomlinson. *Education World®*. Retrieved from http://www.education-world.com/a_issues/ chat/chat107.shtml

Beecher, W. J., & Faxon, G. B., Eds. (1916). *Practical methods, aids, and devices for teachers*, Volume I. Dansville, NY: F.A. Owen Publishing Co.

Bredekamp, S., Copple, C., & Neuman, S. B. (2000). *Learning to read and write: Developmentally appropriate practices for young children*. Washington, DC: The National Association for the Education of Young Children.

Caine, R.N. & Caine, G. (1997). *Education on the edge of possibility*. Virginia: Association for Supervision and Curriculum Development.

Farroni, T., Csibra, G., Simion, F., & Johnson, M. H. (2002). Eye contact detection in humans from birth. *Proceedings of the National Academy of Sciences* USA. 99: 9602–9605.

Gardner, H. (1983). *Frames of mind: The theory in practice*. New York: Basic Books.

Gardner, H. (2000). *Intelligence reframed: Multiple intelligences for the 21st century*. New York: Basic Books.

Grinder, M. (1989). *Righting the educational conveyor belt*. Portland, OR: Metamorphous Press.

Hannaford, C. (1995). Smart moves: *Why learning is not all in your head*. Arlington, VA: Great Oceans Publishers.

Hunter, M. (1994). *Mastery teaching: Increasing instructional effectiveness*. Thousand Oaks, CA: Corwin Press.

Jensen, E. (1997). *Brain compatible strategies*. San Diego, CA: The Brain Store.

Jensen, E. (1998). *Teaching with the brain in mind*. Arlington, VA: Association for Supervision and Curriculum Development.

Professional References

Katz, L. G. (1997, April). A developmental approach to assessment of young children. *ERIC Digest.* Retrieved May 23, 2006 from http://www.kidsource.com/kidsource/content4/assess.development.html

Katz, L. (1999, June). Another look at what young children should be learning. *ERIC Digest.* Retrieved January 13, 2006 from http://ericps.ed.uiuc.edu/eece/pubs/digest

Marcon, R. A. (1995). Fourth-grade slump: The cause and cure. *Principal, 74*(5), 17–20.

Markova, D. (1992). *How your child is smart: A life changing approach to learning.* Berkeley, CA: Conari Press.

Montessori, M. (1986). (Reissue edition.) *Discovery of the Child.* NY: Random House.

National Reading Panel (NRP). (2000). *Teaching children to read: An evidence-based assessment of the scientific research literature on reading and its implications for reading instruction.* Washington, DC: National Institute of Child Health and Development.

O'Meara, S. J. (2002). A little eye music: Stimulation of brain area association with eye-to-eye contact between people. *Odyssey,* 03/01.

Pycha, A. (2000, August). Why practice makes perfect. *BrainConnection.* Retrieved January 31, 2005 from http://www.brainconnection.com/topics/?main=fa/practice

Schweinhart, L. J., & Weikart, D. P. (1997). The High/Scope preschool curriculum comparison study through age 23. *Early Childhood Research Quarterly, 12*(2), 117–43.

Silver, D. (2003). *Drumming to the beat of a different marcher: Finding the rhythm for teaching a differentiated classroom.* Nashville, TN: Incentive Publications.

Tomlinson, C. (1995). *How to differentiate instruction in mixed-ability classrooms.* Alexandria, VA: ASCD.

Children's Literature Cited

Berger, M. (1996). *A butterfly is born*. Northborough, MA: Newbridge Educational Publishers.

Brown, M. (1997). *Stone soup*. New York, NY: Aladdin Picture Books.

Hutchins, P. (1986). *The doorbell rang*. New York, NY: Greenwillow Publishers.

Kraus, R. (1973). *Leo the late bloomer*. New York, NY: HarperCollins Publishers.

Piper, W. (1990). *The little engine that could*. New York, NY: Platt and Munk Publishers.

Feldman, J. (2000). *Sing to learn CD*. Bloomfield Hills, MI: Songs for Teaching.

MacDonald, S. (2004). *A jingle in my pocket CD*. Bloomfield Hills, MI: Songs for Teaching.

Pallotta, J. (1993). *The icky bug alphabet book*. Boston, MA: Charlesbridge Publishers.

Thaler, M. (1982). *Owly*. New York, NY: HarperCollins Children's Books.

Index